Hamlyn all-colour pa

Modern
Combat Aircraft

John W. R. Taylor

illustrated by Mike Codd

Hamlyn
London · New York · Sydney · Toronto

CONTENTS

Published by
The Hamlyn Publishing Group Limited
London · New York
Sydney · Toronto
Astronaut House, Feltham,
Middlesex, England

Copyright © The Hamlyn
Publishing Group Limited 1976
ISBN 0 600 36195 0

Phototypeset by Filmtype Services
Limited, Scarborough
Colour separations by
Metric Reproductions Limited,
Chelmsford, Essex
Printed in Spain by
Mateu Cromo, Madrid

FOREWORD

This is a book about peace, as well as war. In a nuclear age, any major war would be suicidal for both sides, so the primary task of the defence forces of East and West is to pose the threat of such terrible destruction and loss of life that nobody will ever dare to attack his neighbours. This is known as the deterrent policy; it works only as long as each side fears the other's military capability. The weapons available to East and West must not only be equally formidable, they must be *seen* to be capable of doing their job.

Reconnaissance – the earliest task performed by military aircraft before they began carrying guns and bombs as routine – is as vital as ever. Satellites in orbit, and aeroplanes, are in action every second of every day and night, photographing and counting the long-range missiles and combat aircraft deployed by the armed forces of the great powers, identifying every one precisely, learning the capabilities of defensive and missile guidance radars, and watching for the slightest sign of what might be preparation for a surprise attack.

If the missiles and long-range bombers were ever sent into action, loaded to the gunwales with nuclear weapons, the last great battle of Armageddon would have been lost already. Until we discover an infinitely better and less costly alternative, it is the price we must pay for continued survival. Only smaller wars still have to be fought because nobody is willing to risk annihilation by using nuclear weapons to end them quickly. That is why so many different types of military aircraft continue to be needed.

J.W.R.T.

Note: The speed of high-performance aircraft is normally quoted in relation to the speed of sound, which varies with temperature and altitude. The speed of sound, referred to as Mach 1, is approximately 760 mph (1,223 km/h) at sea level in International Standard Atmosphere conditions, dropping progressively to 660 mph (1,062 km/h) in the rarefied atmosphere above 36,000 ft (11,000 m). Thus Mach 2·1 at 40,000 ft (12,200 m) would be equivalent to 2.1 × 660 (1,062), or 1,386 mph (2,230 km/h).

WHAT IS MODERN AIR POWER ?

One-third of the Triad

The piloted bomber is one of three weapons of vast destructive power that make up what America's Department of Defense refers to as the Triad. The others are the intercontinental ballistic missile (ICBM) and the submarine-launched ballistic missile (SLBM). All three are capable of delivering thermonuclear warheads on to distant targets, and of penetrating the best defences that science can devise.

Combat aeroplanes were once considered outmoded in a missile age. ICBM designers began storing rockets in underground concrete launch-tubes, known as silos, with heavy covers to withstand nuclear blast. SLBMs were loaded into fast, deep-diving, nuclear-powered submarines which slipped out of harbour to disappear for weeks or months under the waters that cover nearly three-quarters of the Earth.

Some people question why money must be spent on bombers when long-range missiles can be held at instant readiness for firing, aligned precisely on every key military target in the world. They argue that even if ICBMs are not completely invulnerable, because the positions of their silos can be pinpointed, there are still the SLBMs hidden beneath the ocean. And although both the USA and Soviet Union have perfected anti-ballistic missiles (ABMs) able to intercept ICBM and SLBM warheads, the cost of installing such defences is so crippling that these nations have agreed to limit to 200 the number of ABMs that each will deploy.

Nonetheless, the advent of the ABM meant that no missile could be guaranteed to reach its target intact. Nor could missiles be launched and recalled, like bombers, if a political crisis were resolved at the last minute. They lack the flexibility of piloted bombers, which can approach their targets from any point of the compass, flying beneath the searching beams of defensive radars and protected by radar jamming devices, and then launch their air-to-surface missiles while still beyond the reach of enemy anti-aircraft missiles.

Although basically a '1955 model', the USAF's B-52 Stratofortress bomber has been updated continuously and remains a formidable vehicle for thermonuclear bombs and missiles

No more big formations

In 1914–18 the sky over the battlefield in France was often full of wheeling, zooming, diving aircraft, raking each other with machine-gun bullets during dogfights which created legendary aces such as Richthofen, Mannock and Rickenbacker. In the Second World War a major air raid, by day or night, involved up to one thousand multi-engined bombers, protected by swarms of fighters which flew close escort or ranged far beyond the attacking force, drawing away and engaging enemy interceptors.

Modern nuclear weapons and advanced electronic aids have ended the need for large formations. A single bomber can be guided unerringly in flight by self-contained navigation systems, and can wipe its target off the map with one missile or bomb.

In the same way, a single reconnaissance aircraft can photograph 60,000 square miles (155,000 km^2) of territory in one hour, and identify electronically every type of radar and missile on the ground beneath it. Passing high overhead, at three times the speed of sound, it may not even be detected by the defences.

Vapour trails give away the position of an aircraft flying at the same height as the average jet airliner; at extreme heights, where the latest reconnaissance aircraft fly, there are no vapour trails

RAF Phantoms ensure that a Tu-95 does not stray into British airspace

When an intruder is located in peacetime, fighters are 'scrambled' to investigate it. These RAF Phantoms are keeping watch on one of the Soviet Tu-95s that fly frequently round the North Cape of Norway and over the North Sea, packed with electronics to probe the secrets of NATO defences. The bomber might dive to low altitude where Phantoms burn their fuel more quickly, so a Victor tanker stands by to refuel the fighters in flight.

F-14A Tomcat launches a missile against a target drone

Training the men

In an age when one or two fighters or bombers do the work of hundreds of their predecessors, the men who fly them must be fit and superbly trained. To test their skill, fighter crews are matched against tiny pilotless target drones, which can fly as fast as combat aeroplanes and are able to make tight turns that would 'black out' human pilots. Often the drones carry devices which make them appear as large as bombers on a fighter radar screen, and jammers to confuse the fighter's radar.

One US Navy fighter crew, flying an F-14A Tomcat, located a Firebee II drone 126 miles (203 km) away, coming towards them at Mach 1·55 at a height of 52,000 ft (15,850 m). The Tomcat was flying at Mach 1·45 at 45,000 ft (13,700 m). Although the drone was using jammers, a Phoenix missile launched from the fighter had no difficulty in tracking it and passing by so closely that it would have destroyed the Firebee had it been fitted with a live warhead.

Firing guns and missiles against drones or dropping bombs on practice ranges is one kind of advanced training. Another, enjoyed each year by millions of spectators as well as by the pilots, is the kind of precision formation flying displayed at air shows by military teams like the RAF Red Arrows and USAF Thunderbirds. To people on the ground, loops and rolls in formation with the aircraft's wingtips and cockpit canopies separated by a few feet seem almost suicidal. For the pilots, the flying skill and discipline enhanced by such displays could make the difference between life and death one day, in a wartime or peacetime emergency.

Combat formations are smaller nowadays, but no less essential because they help each man to protect his neighbours as well as himself during an attack by enemy interceptors. In place of the once normal symmetrical V, the pattern favoured by most modern air forces is 'finger four', with the aircraft positioned as the fingertips of a hand placed flat on the table.

Gnat Trainers flown by the Red Arrows, one of the world's most renowned formation aerobatic teams

Racing against time, a British Army Scout helicopter snatches a
trapped man from the roof of a burning tower block

Training can sometimes be combined with life-saving, and
countless thousands of people are alive today because military
aircrews came to their aid when nothing else could have helped
them. Some incidents are spectacular – as when more than 400
people were snatched from the top of a burning 25-storey
building by a dozen helicopters in Sao Paulo, Brazil. More
often, the rescue attempts go unnoticed, because it is no longer
news when a small and very frightened boy is hoisted out of
a rubber boat that was drifting out to sea off a holiday beach,
or when an injured climber is plucked from a mountain ledge.

Helicopters are unrivalled for such work. Typical operations
involved Sea Kings of the Royal Navy and German Navy which
saved 35 people from two major shipwrecks in severe storms
off the south-west coast of England in less than a month. After

long flights to where the ships had foundered, the helicopters had to hover above 70 ft (21 m) waves, battered by winds of up to 100 mph (160 km/h) in continuously driving salt spray, to perform their rescues.

Where it is possible to make a normal take-off and landing, or where loads can be dropped by parachute, it is often better to use fixed-wing aeroplanes. When famine threatened drought-stricken Mali, in Africa, two RAF Hercules transports flew 15 hours a day repeatedly to deliver 2,500 tons of life-saving grain. It was the fifth mission of its kind performed by the RAF in a period of eight months.

Airdropping food from a USAF Hercules during famine in a mountain area

STRATEGIC ATTACK

Almost every military aeroplane starts life as an operational requirement. The air staff decides that one particular type of aircraft will no longer be good enough to do its assigned job in, say, seven years' time. So they draw up a specification of the kind of aircraft that will be needed, and send it to those companies with the necessary competence and experience to compete for a contract to build the aircraft.

Let us assume that the specification is for a new bomber or strike aircraft. The specification will outline whether the aircraft is expected to make its attack at high or low altitude; whether its maximum speed is to be above the structural limit for aluminium, requiring special steels, titanium and non-metallic composites; whether it is intended to operate alone, or will need an escort of fighters or specialised ECM (electronic countermeasures) radar jamming aircraft; whether it must be equipped for all-weather operation, by day and night; whether its weapon load will consist of 'iron bombs', nuclear bombs or long-range air-to-surface missiles; and whether it must carry

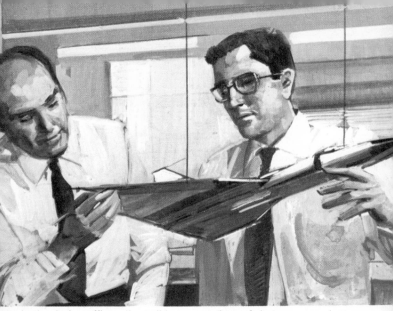

In the design office, all possible permutations of shape, power plant, performance and weapons for the new aircraft are compared

penetration aids such as defensive guns or rockets, or decoy missiles able to produce the same 'blip' as the aircraft itself on enemy radar screens, to confuse the defences.

There will be further requests for detailed time and cost estimates to ensure that the aircraft can be ready when needed, and within a restricted defence budget.

The chief engineer of each company has to select the best configuration to meet the conflicting dictates of high performance and low cost, structural strength and light weight, and elaborate equipment for almost-automatic missions versus ease of maintenance and reliability. Discussions go on for months. Models tested in wind tunnels reveal how closely any design will meet performance requirements. Full-scale mock-ups are built, so detailed that they do everything but fly. Simulators, consisting of dummy cockpits with controls and instruments linked to computers, indicate precisely how each design will handle in the air.

While the air staff's technical experts assess the test reports and performance predictions received from companies competing to build their new aircraft, the old bombers get older . . .

US President Theodore Roosevelt, at the beginning of our century, said that the way to keep the peace was to 'speak softly and carry a big stick'. The big stick of the US Air Force in the mid-seventies is still the eight-engined B-52 Stratofortress, first flown in 1952.

Boeing began developing this 200-ton strategic bomber in mid-1945, before the first atomic bombs were dropped on Japan. A total of 744 B-52s were delivered, in seven operational versions, before production ended in 1962. Able to cruise at just below the speed of sound, at a height of 50,000 ft (15,250 m), they did not need the bristling defensive armament of wartime bombers, although the original versions retained a tail-gunner's position. This could be reached by a crawlway from the main crew compartment only when the aircraft was not pressurised for high-altitude flight. Most of the time the gunner lived in his own little world, 50 yards (45 m) from the other crew-members, complete with an electric stove, toilet and other home comforts.

B-52B, an early version of the Stratofortress with taller tail-fin and smaller underwing auxiliary fuel tanks than those fitted to later models

Tupolev Tu-95, the world's fastest propeller-driven combat aircraft

Russia's counterpart to the B-52 was the four-jet Myasish-chev M-4, first displayed in a fly-past over Moscow in 1954. In the following year, a second Soviet strategic bomber put in an appearance in the shape of the Tupolev Tu-95, which was allocated the NATO reporting name of 'Bear'. Up to this time, everyone considered that 425 mph (685 km/h) was about as fast as a propeller-driven aeroplane would ever fly. It came as a shock, therefore, to learn that the turboprop-powered Tu-95 could exceed 500 mph (805 km/h) and had a range of 7,800 miles (12,550 km) with 11 tons of bombs. Only the fact that its operating height was limited to 41,000 ft (12,500 m) by its propellers reflected that it was not a high-flying jet and so needed three gun turrets, each mounting two 23 mm cannon, to beat off attacking fighters.

Because of the high cost and complexity of modern military aircraft, few nations can afford to operate a force of long-range strategic bombers designed to destroy an enemy's ability and will to continue fighting by mounting a persistent, methodical offensive against his homeland.

A D.H.9 bomber of the First World War cost £2,562, plus machine-guns and a few simple instruments. Its weight, complete with crew, fuel and weapons, was a mere 3,503 lb (1,589 kg). By comparison, some modern airframes cost more than their weight in gold and the bombs and missiles carried by a single B-1 are equivalent in weight to two whole squadrons of fully-loaded D.H.9s. It is easy to understand why such aircraft must be both costly and complex . . .

To give a bomber or strike aircraft of the 'seventies sufficient range to reach distant targets, it must be able to refuel in flight. This requires either a probe through which to take in fuel transferred by a hose trailed from a tanker 'plane, or a receptacle for the rigid 'flying boom' refuelling system favoured by the US Air Force.

Refuelling probes are usually mounted on the nose of the receiving aircraft above a dielectric nosecone housing a large radar. This radar performs a whole range of tasks. As a start, it checks navigation by providing the crew with a moving map display of the terrain over which they pass during the long journey towards their target – a part of the mission normally flown at high altitude to conserve fuel. It can warn of bad weather, aircraft or high ground ahead, and can cause an IFF (identification, friend or foe) set to interrogate any unidentified aircraft, triggering an automatic 'friendly' response if the latter is not hostile. After positive identification of an enemy, it can launch defensive missiles automatically.

1 B-52H Stratofortress launching one of its 20 AGM-86A Air-Launched Cruise Missiles, which are turbofan-powered and carry a nuclear warhead
2 The box at the tip of the Vulcan's tail-fin contains ECM equipment. Other jamming and defensive devices fill the bulged tailcone
3 Turrets under the nose of this B-52H house steerable FLIR and LLLTV sensors, giving the crew improved 'night eyes'
4 The nose of this late-model Myasishchev M-4 (NATO 'Bison-C') has a refuelling probe and large search radar forward of the visual bomb-aiming position
5 Another Soviet bomber with nose refuelling probe and large radome is this version of the Tu-95 (NATO 'Bear-C')

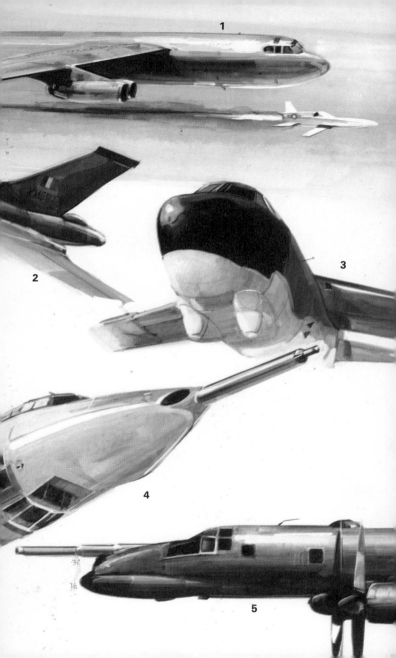

A B-1 flying low with its wings fully swept. With a speed of Mach 1·6 and 115,000 lb (52,160 kg) weapon load, it costs about $80 million. The USAF wants 244 B-1s

As in the case of an airliner, the bomber can be flown by its automatic pilot almost continually from take-off to touchdown, leaving the crew free to concentrate on tactics. Before leaving the ground, the pilot simply ensures that the co-ordinates of the target are fed into a computer which then guides the air-craft unerringly by means of self-contained, unjammable, inertial and Doppler navigation systems linked to the auto-pilot. If a roundabout course is safer than a direct flight, the necessary intermediate turning points are also fed in.

Even if the approach to the target has to be made at a height of less than 500 ft (150 m) to reduce the possibility of detection by ground radar, the aircraft's own radar can remain in con-trol in what is called terrain-following mode. Measuring height above the surface extremely rapidly and accurately, it guides the aircraft over or between hills and mountains and

down the other side. Even if it develops a fault, the risk of accident is averted by a fail-safe mechanism which puts the aircraft automatically into a steep climb.

Modern defence systems are so efficient that few attacks remain undetected for long. Passive ECM (electronic counter-measures) equipment, housed perhaps in a box on the tail-fin, warns the crew when the bomber is being tracked by radar on the ground – perhaps at a missile launch site – or in an enemy interceptor. Active ECM jammers can then be switched on to prevent the enemy from locating the bomber, or strips of metalised paper known as 'chaff' can be dropped to produce a cluttered, completely useless, picture on the enemy radar screens.

As the target approaches, the aircraft's main radar can ensure that its missiles or bombs are released at the precise point when they will achieve the best results. When carrying long-range air-to-surface missiles, the bomber need never venture near to the target's close defences. Launching its weapons hundreds of miles away, it can turn for home and safety long before they reach the ground.

The pilot can take control, overriding the autopilot, at any second if he so wishes. He can launch small decoy missiles, indistinguishable from his bomber on enemy radar screens. If he is flying a B-52, a forward-looking infra-red (FLIR) scanner and a low-light-level TV camera, mounted in undernose blisters, will help him to see where he is going at night or in bad weather while flying at treetop height.

By adding such devices to ageing aircraft, their useful life-time can be extended by many years. However, the time for retirement must come eventually, either because the aircraft have been flown for so many thousands of hours that the metals from which their airframe is made have become fatigued and lost their strength, or because they are no longer good enough to penetrate improved enemy defences.

The B-1 is the logical replacement for the B-52 as far as the USAF is concerned, but that does not prevent America's Department of Defense from studying alternatives that might increase the effectiveness of the Triad or reduce its cost. In October 1974, an obsolete Minuteman I ICBM was dragged by parachute out of the open rear loading door of a C-5 Galaxy transport flying over the Pacific Test Range. As the missile dropped towards the sea, its first-stage motor was ignited for ten seconds and it climbed to 20,000 ft (6,100 m), proving that an ICBM could be air-launched from a difficult-to-locate air-craft as an alternative to ground launching from an easy-to-pinpoint silo.

This could lead to new interest in air-launched ballistic missiles like Skybolt, which was intended to be carried by B-52 and British Vulcan bombers but was abandoned as too costly in 1962. It could also make aircraft like the Boeing 747 'Jumbo', with a large cabin for ICBMs, ideal as tomorrow's bombers. They would certainly be more difficult to locate and destroy than any silo-housed missile and could be deployed more quickly, to a wider choice of targets, than a missile-launching submarine. Whether they could replace aircraft like the B-1 is more debatable.

Air-launching an ICBM from a projected military version of the DC-10 airliner

TACTICAL ATTACK

Unlike strategic bombers, designed to obliterate targets deep inside enemy territory, tactical attack aircraft normally operate over battle areas near their own airfields. Their bases may have to be built hurriedly to keep pace with an advancing army for which they are providing close support. This means that such aircraft must be able to take off and land on small, rough airstrips and be kept serviceable without the elaborate ground equipment available at permanent airfields.

They do not need to carry the heaviest bombs and air-to-surface missiles as their targets are seldom large. On the other hand, they should, ideally, carry a very large number of bombs, rockets, missiles and even tactical nuclear weapons, suitable for attacking a variety of targets, without having to keep returning to base to re-arm every few minutes. Their pilots must be able to find the targets, whatever the conditions – even when these are highly mobile vehicles such as tanks and small naval craft. Having found them, the attacking aircraft must be sufficiently manoeuvrable to dodge ground fire and missiles, and to outfly enemy fighters. Nor are they likely to survive for long unless their cockpit, engine, fuel system and other key areas are armoured against hits by small arms fire.

No single type of aircraft could begin to meet all these requirements. Even the character of the opposition can range from a vast war machine, equipped with the most sophisticated weapons, to a small band of terrorists in a jungle, carrying only personal arms and living off the land.

For these and other reasons, attack aircraft are built in an astonishing variety of shapes and sizes. At one extreme is the $20 million, Mach 2·5, swing-wing American F-111. The Yugoslav Kraguj is as different as it could be, comprising little more than a cheap-to-build, easy-to-fly lightplane, able to fly from small grass fields to attack lightly-armed insurgents with 220 lb (100 kg) bombs, rockets and machine-gun fire.

Opposite top The Kraguj was designed as an inexpensive attack aircraft which even a civilian lightplane pilot could learn to fly in a short time
Bottom Very different from the Kraguj, the swing-wing F-111 can fly at Mach 2·5 and carry seven tons of weapons

Although intended primarily for daylight use, the A-10 might take advantage of the half-light of dawn or dusk to attack a heavily defended target

Aircraft like the Kraguj are intended to fly low, taking advantage of every scrap of natural cover from trees and hills, to catch by surprise small groups of men or vehicles on the ground. Unfortunately, even guerrilla bands often have light-weight, shoulder-fired anti-aircraft missiles such as the Russian SA-7, ready for almost instant use and fitted with an infra-red heat-seeker which homes on the aircraft's engine exhaust.

All kinds of aircraft have been fitted with weapons in an effort to find an inexpensive, all-purpose tactical attacker. Retired trainers and piston-engined combat types like the American T-28 and A-1 Skyraider did good work during the early years in Vietnam. Armed versions of jet trainers are far more effective, at greater cost (see pages 56–63). Even veteran C-47 (Dakota) piston-engined transports were fitted with six-barrel Miniguns so that they could circle over suspected enemy troop positions in Vietnam, pouring a vast hail of fire towards the ground. The results were so spectacular that similar gunship conversions of the C-119 Flying Boxcar and four-turboprop C-130 Hercules followed.

No longer simple or cheap, the AC-130H Hercules gunship carried a huge 105 mm howitzer, a 40 mm cannon, two 20 mm cannon, two Miniguns, a searchlight and a whole range of infra-red, TV and laser devices which enabled it to locate its targets precisely by day or night in all weathers.

On the basis of this experience, the USAF ordered in the mid-seventies a unique, specialised attack aircraft known as the Fairchild A-10. High speed was sacrificed for economy, quietness, long range, survivability and extremely heavy armament. Two 9,065 lb (4,112 kg) thrust TF34 turbofan engines give the A-10 a maximum speed of 453 mph (729 km/h) and the ability to carry 9,500 lb (4,300 kg) of weapons 290 miles (465 km) from its base and then spend two hours over the battle area seeking out targets. Maximum weapon load is 16,000 lb (7,250 kg) – about four times the average bomb-load carried by American four-engined heavy bombers in the Second World War. The pilot sits in a 'bathtub' of armour plate and has a 30 mm multi-barrel cannon to keep the defences quiet.

Destroying bridges is more difficult than it looks. Bombs or missiles have to be aimed very precisely to hit and destroy a support or span; and the enemy usually emplaces formidable anti-aircraft defences around such vital targets.

Racing in low towards a bridge, the pilot of an F-4E Phantom II carrying laser-guided bombs knows that by himself he would have little chance of success. Somewhere above, an aircraft packed with ECM jammers is doing its best to confuse the defenders' warning radars and to prevent enemy missiles 'locking on' to the incoming raiders. Under the wing of his aircraft, a TV camera in the nose of a torpedo-shape container known as Pave Spike has already begun to display a picture of the bridge on a screen in the rear cockpit.

Carefully, the weapons system operator steers the camera so that a cross-hair sight on the screen is centred on one of the bridge supports. To see it more clearly, he enlarges this part of the picture by remote focusing of the lens. Now the camera is locked on the support and will hold its aim even if the aircraft has to manoeuvre to provide a more difficult target for ground fire. A laser designator, aligned precisely with the TV camera, has begun transmitting a narrow laser beam on to the exact

Two laser-guided weapons, launched from an F-4 Phantom II, speed towards a target 'illuminated' by a laser designator operated by ground forces on a nearby hillside

An A-7D Corsair II starts to climb away after destroying an enemy bridge in a dive attack with simple 'iron bombs'

point on the bridge support that the weapons system operator selected with his cross-hair sight.

(If there had been friendly troops near the bridge, Pave Spike would not have been needed. Instead, one of the men on the ground would have directed a laser designator on the bridge support. The result would be the same.)

The time taken for the laser beam from Pave Spike to reach the target tells the fighter's crew the distance to the bridge.

As they close the gap at almost the speed of sound, a laser receiver on the nose of each of the bombs under the Phantom's wings has already locked on to the spot on the bridge 'illuminated' by the designator. At exactly the right range, the bombs are released and the pilot pulls up into a bone-crushing climbing turn for home as they race down to smash the bridge.

This is sophisticated computer-age warfare, with science helping the aircrews to achieve results that would have seemed quite impossible during the Second World War, especially in the face of determined defences. But there is still a place for old-fashioned flying skill.

This was proved in Vietnam by the USAF's 354th Tactical Fighter Wing, equipped with single-seat LTV A-7D Corsair IIs. During the last ten weeks of US involvement in the war, the Wing's 72 aircraft dropped nearly 25,000 bombs, most of them 500-pounders, with an estimated average miss distance of ten metres. Only two A-7s were lost in action.

One mission was described by a pilot as follows: 'When our flight of three A-7s got to the target area in Laos, three F-4s were working it with laser-guided bombs. They were going after a bridge and had damaged it extensively before their fuel ran low and they had to leave. Then the forward air controller (FAC) put us on the bridge. One of our pilots was a first lieutenant on his second mission in south-east Asia – the second time he had ever dropped bombs in combat. We destroyed that bridge with three bombs.

'Next the FAC gave us a bypass bridge about 100 metres down river. We dropped it with two bombs and went over to a ferry crossing on another river. With three bombs, we destroyed the ferry cable, the dock and the ferry. The FAC said he had only one more bridge. We went down to it and destroyed it with three bombs.'

Such results, achieved usually from an altitude of 5,000 to 7,000 ft (well above most enemy ground fire), led to a serious review of US plans for future attack aircraft. The end product is the A-10.

Behind the small windows in the nose of this RAF Jaguar is a laser rangefinder which can measure the distance to a target on the ground, and a marked target seeker which picks up any target 'illuminated' by a laser designator

In Europe and the Soviet Union, there is little confidence in aircraft as slow as the A-10. The RAF and French Air Force believe that high speed and small size offer a better hope of survival in the heavily defended front-line area. Their thinking is epitomised in the Jaguar, a mini-attacker with a maxi-punch. Built in partnership by British and French companies, it spans a mere 28 ft 6 in (8·69 m). This is less than the span of America's F-16 lightweight fighter, and its maximum loaded weight of 34,000 lb (15,500 kg) is 5 tons less than that of the A-10. Yet the Jaguar can fly at Mach 1·5 at height. At sea level, it can race to the target at supersonic speed carrying up to 10,000 lb (4,500 kg) of attack weapons.

Jaguar is fitted with ECM and a laser target seeker, to ensure accuracy of delivery, but lacks the radar equipment necessary for night operations. Radar increases an aircraft's size, weight and cost, and every extra pound of equipment fitted to an

The Soviet MiG-23 swing-wing fighter-bomber is also in service as an interceptor armed with air-to-air missiles

Terrain-following radar in the MRCA enables it to seek the cover of mountains en route to its target even while it is flying under automatic control

aeroplane means one less pound of fuel or weapons. Most heavy combat aircraft also require long paved runways from which to fly and this prevents them from using hastily prepared airstrips in front-line areas.

Fitting of low-pressure tyres sometimes permits the use of grass strips, while take-off runs can be reduced and loads increased by fitting 'variable-geometry' swing-wings. Spread for take-off and landing, these reduce the length of runway required and enable heavier loads to be carried. Pivoted back for high-speed flight, they offer the high-speed characteristics of a swept or delta wing.

First entirely successful swing-wing aircraft (though not without serious problems at first) was the USAF's General Dynamics F-111 tactical fighter. Russia next found a way of increasing the pathetically poor range of its Su-7 fighter-bomber by pivoting just the outer sections of each wing, to produce the Su-17 and Su-20, before putting into service the more advanced MiG-23 and Su-19, known to NATO as 'Flogger' and 'Fencer' respectively.

Europe's counterpart is the MRCA, or multi-role combat aircraft, developed in partnership by British, German and Italian companies. Although comparatively small it carries a huge weapon load, including two 27 mm guns, can fly at Mach 2, and has all the radar, ECM and other equipment needed for low-level operations around the clock.

Without a swing-wing and the very latest equipment, the MRCA would never have done its job. Small size and the shared costs of the three-nation programme have made it practicable for the RAF alone to plan the purchase of 385 aircraft in the late 1970s and early 1980s. Some will replace four-jet Vulcans for overland strike and reconnaissance; others will re-equip Buccaneer attack and maritime squadrons. Eventually, MRCAs will even take over air defence duties from Phantoms. So the term 'multi-role' is no exaggeration.

If any further proof were needed that Europe can still design combat aircraft second to none, Britain's Hawker Siddeley Harrier would provide it. Dubbed a 'jump-jet' by the press, this remarkable little attack/reconnaissance aircraft was the first fixed-wing type to offer the go-anywhere versatility of a helicopter. Key to this is its Rolls-Royce Pegasus vectored-thrust engine, from which the exhaust gases are ejected through four swivelling nozzles. Turning these downward enables the Harrier to take off and land vertically, and hover. By turning them part-way, the aircraft becomes a short take-off and landing (STOL) rather than a vertical take-off and landing (VTOL) type, carrying a heavier load.

The Harrier can operate from fields, roads, factory yards, platforms on ships, or anywhere large enough and firm enough to take it. It can be hidden under trees or camouflage nets until take-off time, close to the troops for whom it provides support. Nor is it complicated – the only additional control in the cockpit, compared with a conventional jet, is a lever to rotate the exhaust nozzles.

The vertical take-off Harrier, only fixed-wing combat aircraft with the go-anywhere capability of a helicopter

FIGHTERS

Fighters were once the least complicated of all military aircraft. All they needed were guns to fire at enemy aircraft and some kind of gunsight to ensure accuracy of aim. Bombracks were fitted to many of them before the end of the First World War so that they could attack any 'targets of opportunity' spotted on the ground. Then came oxygen equipment to enable their pilots to fly higher, gyroscopic gunsights, radar to locate and track enemy aircraft at night, and a never-ending succession of other devices to make them more formidable.

Today, a fighter can weigh as much as a four-engined bomber of the Second World War, and carry a bomb load far greater than the average load of a Fortress or Lancaster. Its radar helps with navigation and is often capable of locating an enemy aircraft at night; it flies the fighter automatically towards it, firing the guns or missiles at precisely the right moment to ensure destruction of the enemy, and then puts the fighter in a climbing turn to avoid the wreckage and sets course for home. In daylight, the old-fashioned gunsight is replaced by a head-up display (HUD) which projects on to the pilot's windscreen data on speed, height and other key information, so that he does not need to glance down at his cockpit instruments while lining up on target.

Fighters need ECM devices to help them elude the defences. Some, like the USAF's 'Wild Weasel' version of the Phantom, carry powerful jammers to destroy the effectiveness of enemy warning radars and missile guidance radars. Small infra-red seekers, like Pave Penny fitted to US fighters, detect anything hot, such as the exhaust of an enemy aircraft or the engines of tanks and trucks hidden on the ground. Homing air-to-air and air-to-surface missiles supplement guns, which may themselves have six rotating barrels able to pump out 20 mm shells at rates of fire of up to 6,000 rounds a minute.

The 'Christmas tree' effect of all this equipment is well illustrated by the RAF Phantom opposite. Slung beneath its wings and fuselage are two auxiliary fuel tanks, four rocket

Phantom reconnaissance-fighter of the RAF with a typical load of sensors, rockets, missiles and long-range fuel tanks

The US Navy's F-14A Tomcat swing-wing fighter, with wings fully extended

pods, Sparrow radar-guided air-to-air missiles, and a reconnaissance pod filled with cameras, infra-red sensors and linescan radar which produces photographs of the scene below in all weathers and at night. Combining ground attack, reconnaissance and air combat capabilities in a single aircraft, the Phantom is almost an air force in miniature. Yet even that is not the limit of the Phantom's versatility. The US Navy and Royal Navy operate it at sea from aircraft carriers; it was, in fact, designed originally for naval use and then adapted also for shore-based service.

To replace it, the USAF and US Navy have evolved two very different aircraft. Each has twin engines and the twin tail-fins that designers often prefer to a single, very large fin; but the Navy's F-14A Tomcat is a two-seater with swing-wings, whereas the USAF's F-15A Eagle is a single-seater with a broad Phantom-like fixed wing.

Designed and built by Grumman, the Tomcat is a heavyweight even among modern fighters. Its wings span 64 ft $1\frac{1}{2}$ in

(19·54 m) spread and 38 ft 2 in (11·63 m) swept. It is 62 ft (18·89 m) long, with a maximum loaded weight of 72,000 lb (32,658 kg), and has a top speed of Mach 2·34. Armament includes a 20 mm multi-barrel gun and up to six Phoenix air-to-air missiles or 14,500 lb (6,575 kg) of other weapons such as bombs and rockets.

The Eagle, like the Phantom, is a McDonnell Douglas design. It is 63 ft 9¾ in (19·45 m) long and can carry 12,000 lb (5,443 kg) of ground attack weapons if required. Maximum speed is above Mach 2·5, and a specially prepared F-15A, named *Streak Eagle*, proved its high rate of climb by reaching a height of 30,000 m (98,425 ft) in less than 3½ minutes in February 1975. This is an important capability because neither the Eagle nor the Tomcat is as fast or high-flying as the Soviet MiG-25. As a result they must be able to offset the higher performance of such aircraft by high rate of climb and the great speed, range and accuracy of their air-to-air missiles.

Most 1914–18 fighters were biplanes with a single piston-engine mounted in their nose and with a fixed undercarriage. By the Second World War the standard configuration was a

F-15A Eagle of the USAF with its over-fuselage airbrake partly open to slow it. Four Sparrow air-to-air missiles are mounted on the lower edges of its engine air intake ducts

low-wing monoplane, with a much more powerful nose-mounted engine and retractable undercarriage. Today, every fighter design team seems to have its own ideas on the best layout for its products, and spotters have few of the identification problems that beset members of organisations like the Royal Observer Corps in 1939–45.

No aircraft demonstrate this variety of shape better than those built by the Saab-Scania company in Sweden. In the mid-1950s, after extensive wind-tunnel research, Saab evolved what it called the 'double-delta' planform for its J 35 Draken single-seater. This proved to be a fine fighter, with a speed of Mach 2 in its final form, which was still in production 20 years after the first flight of the prototype.

Nevertheless, Saab's designers felt sure that they could do even better. Asked to evolve a new combat aircraft for the Swedish Air Force that would be suitable for attack, interception and armed reconnaissance missions, they went back to the drawing board and wind tunnel and came up this time with a tandem delta.

The aircraft required by the Swedish Air Force had to fly at Mach 2 and carry a heavy load of weapons. Designed around an afterburning version of an American Pratt & Whitney engine developing 26,000 lb (11,800 kg) of thrust, its loaded weight could not be less than 35,000 lb (15,875 kg), yet it had to be able to operate from the stretches of main road that Sweden uses for combat airstrips.

By fitting flaps to the forward delta, the Swedish engineers found that they could give their new design STOL capability – and so was born the Viggen, one of the great military aircraft of the present era. First version to enter service was the AJ 37, armed with air-to-surface missiles. It was followed by the photo-reconnaissance SF 37 and sea surveillance SH 37, with the JA 37 interceptor under development for service in the late 1970s.

French designers do not share all the problems of the Swedes, whose nation is mere minutes away from potential invaders. With more time to detect and intercept an attacking force,

The tandem-delta Viggen taking off from a road base, a type of combat strip used in Sweden

Israeli Mirage III attacking an Egyptian airfield in the air strike which heralded the start of the Six-Day War in 1967

they do not need to use such high power to climb to a great height in minimum time. With a greater land area, they need not design aircraft that will operate from roads; the ability to fly from large fields is sufficient insurance against attacks on French regular air bases.

The Mirage III and Mirage 5 delta-wing fighters reflect these more modest demands. Easy to fly and service, they have been bought by the air forces of 18 nations. Less experienced countries use their aircraft in only fair-weather conditions; but the Mirage can be as sophisticated as the customer wishes, with a fire control system to handle its guns and missiles and a semi-automatic navigation system. This utilises plastic punch-cards, each representing the geographical co-ordinates of a place along the route to and from the target, the target itself, the home airfield and alternative airfields. The compass heading and distance to successive points is presented to the pilot automatically and continuously in flight. Relieved of navigation chores, he can devote all his attention to tactics.

With a top speed of Mach 2·2 and the ability to operate in

interceptor, ground attack or reconnaissance roles, the Mirage III and 5 have continued in production for 15 years. Their destructive power has been demonstrated repeatedly by the Israelis, whose Mirages played a leading part in the surprise attacks which eliminated opposing Arab air forces at the start of the 1967 Six-Day War. But even the best aircraft cannot last for ever.

Seeking a replacement for the Mirage delta, Dassault switched to a swept wing and tail on the Mirage F1, which became operational with the French Air Force in 1974. This fighter can fly at Mach 2·2, take off in a shorter distance than even a Mirage III, and better the latter's manoeuvrability by 80 per cent, although its engine gives only 15,875 lb (7,200 kg) of thrust – less than one-third the engine power of America's F-15 Eagle.

Only nations like the United States and oil-rich Iran can afford to buy large numbers of fighters in the class of the F-14 and F-15, costing respectively $17 million and $15 million each. This helps to explain the success of the French Mirage III, which can be bought for about one-tenth of such sums.

The swept-wing Mirage F1, which can take off in a shorter distance than the Mirage III, has better manoeuvrability and can fly further

MiG-21 pulling a tight turn to elude a Sidewinder missile. Combat experience has shown that few existing missiles can home on an aircraft as agile as this, and most countries are seeking more manoeuvrable 'dogfight' missiles

Through the years, a few engineers have tried to convince air forces that it is better to have a vast number of small, low-cost fighters than a handful of aircraft that cost a king's ransom and can be flown only by college graduates. One such man was 'Teddy' Petter, best known as the designer of the English Electric Canberra jet bomber. In the early 'fifties, he conceived for the Folland company a miniature fighter called the Gnat, spanning about 22 ft (6·76 m) and powered by a Bristol Orpheus turbojet of only 4,520 lb (2,050 kg) thrust. This remarkable little aircraft proved able to fly at the speed of sound, was armed with two 30 mm cannon and could carry bombs or rockets under its wings. The RAF was interested only in a training version, but India decided to build Gnats at Bangalore and has used them successfully in combat against far more sophisticated fighters such as the F-104 Starfighter and MiG-19.

It is seldom appreciated that the majority of Soviet fighters are lightweights. The MiG-21 delta spans only 23 ft 5½ in (7·15 m) and weighs less than half as much as an American F-4 Phantom or F-15 Eagle. Early versions had a radar of limited effectiveness, and carried light armament and sufficient fuel for only a modest range; but performance and armament have improved with each successive new model.

The MiG-21 of the mid-seventies, flown by more than 20 air forces, has a top speed of Mach 2·1, a far more capable radar, extra fuel, and an armament that includes a twin-barrel 23 mm gun, plus four air-to-air missiles or a variety of bombs and rockets. It is a real 'pilot's aeroplane', which can be delivered to countries as inexperienced with jet fighters as Bangladesh and Tanzania. And its small size enables it to get out of trouble by pulling very tight turns to elude less agile opponents.

In 1972, General Dynamics and Northrop were each awarded a contract to build two prototype lightweight fighters. These aircraft were not intended to be future combat types. Instead, the designers were encouraged to build into their prototypes every bright new idea that might improve the efficiency of a

Dogfight: Gnat v Starfighter. At low altitude, the tiny Gnat has proved itself as good as any opposition

fighter while, at the same time, keeping size, complexity and cost to a minimum.

The programme produced two such remarkable designs that the USAF announced, in mid-1974, that it might buy up to 650 of the most suitable type as an inexpensive partner for the F-15 Eagle.

First to fly, on 20 January that year, had been the General Dynamics YF-16, with a single Pratt & Whitney F100-PW-100 afterburning turbofan engine which gave the aircraft a thrust-to-weight ratio of about 1·5 to 1 at normal combat weight. The promise of a speed in excess of Mach 2, a truly phenomenal rate of climb and superb manoeuvrability was quickly fulfilled. The pilot, reclining 30 degrees, controlled the aircraft by means of a side stick that moved only a fraction of an inch in any direction, generating 'fly-by-wire' electrical signals to move the control surfaces, with none of the usual vulnerable steel cables or rods. He could 'pull' up to 9g in tight turns without blacking out, and firing trials showed the aircraft to be a stable weapon platform.

The first Northrop YF-17 flew on 9 June 1974, displaying as many advanced features as the YF-16 but very different in

General Dynamics YF-16 air combat fighter, chosen by four NATO air forces in Europe as well as by the USAF

Northrop YF-17, a slightly enlarged version of which will be operated by the US Navy as the F-18

concept. As a start, it was larger, twin-tailed, and had two General Electric YJ101 afterburning turbojets giving a total of 30,000 lb (13,600 kg) thrust. Extended wing-root leading-edges, containing slots, offered much increased lift, reduced drag and improved handling. Performance was in the same class as that of the YF-16; Northrop argued that twin engines offered better 'get-you-home' safety than one and that the larger fuselage provided more room for combat radar, equipment, and the second seat in a planned trainer version.

In January 1975, the USAF chose the YF-16 as its new air combat fighter. Although Congress had ruled that the US Navy should have the same fighter as the Air Force to save time and money, the Navy selected a McDonnell Douglas/Northrop development of the YF-17, redesignated F-18.

HELICOPTERS

One of the most important dates in aviation history is 13 May 1940, when Igor Sikorsky made the first untethered flight in his VS-300 helicopter. There had been earlier, successful rotating-wing aircraft, but none had matched the lightweight simplicity of the VS-300, which represented the starting point of the helicopter industry.

Sikorsky was a gentle genius who believed that his aircraft would make life better for the world. Its ability to take off and land vertically almost anywhere, and to hover, made it the most versatile transport vehicle ever devised, and opened up immense possibilities as a means of rescue for people in danger on mountains, sinking ships, and other places beyond the reach of normal aid. But there was war in Europe in 1940 and before long production aircraft evolved from the VS-300 were being sent to sea to discover if they could locate and attack the submarines that were a major threat to Allied survival.

The war ended before the early helicopters, with their limited load-carrying ability, could make any real impact as military aircraft. Their nickname of 'choppers' reflected the distinctive beat of their scything rotors in flight rather than anything more sinister. Even when they proved their capability as front-line transports in Korea, in the early 'fifties, by dropping men, guns and supplies on mountains, they were unarmed. Igor Sikorsky could be well pleased because the same helicopters, many of them built by his company, evacuated casualties to where they could be treated quickly. This reduced the death rate for wounded men to the lowest percentage in military history.

By the time America became involved in another war, in Vietnam, the helicopter was firmly established as a normal means of transporting troops quickly. The little two-seat Sikorsky R-4s of the Second World War, and the twelve-seat H-19s used in Korea, had given way to much larger types able to carry fully-equipped companies of troops, ready for immediate action the moment they touched ground. The helicopter was no longer a vehicle which enemies could allow to

Reloading the rocket pod of a UH-1A Iroquois, the first widely used armed escort helicopter

Piasecki H-21 troop-carrier and a Bell UH-1 Iroquois fitted with anti-tank missiles and rockets

come and go unopposed, and 'chopper' was soon to have a different meaning.

Not all military leaders were enthusiastic about the use of helicopters in combat areas. Engine and rotor noise usually made a surprise attack impossible, even when the aircraft flew low to take advantage of every scrap of natural cover until they reached their drop-zones. It was also widely believed that a helicopter rotor was so delicately balanced that a hit on one blade would cause the aircraft to crash.

It was soon apparent from experience in Vietnam that helicopters could absorb considerable damage and get home safely; but the enemy became increasingly aggressive. North Vietnamese and Vietcong could sometimes guess the area where 'choppers' would try to disembark their loads, and lie in wait to fire on the aircraft and troops the moment they were on the ground. Casualties began to increase alarmingly and it was clear that the airborne assault forces had to be provided with some form of protection.

Normal forms of close support, even by the older, slower types of attack aircraft then being used in Vietnam, were not practicable. The difference in speed between the fixed-wing and rotating-wing machines was still so great that synchronization of arrival over a drop-zone was difficult, even when combat aircraft could be spared for such escort duties. Nor was it easy to locate the well-hidden enemy from an aeroplane that could not hover.

The answer was to arm the helicopter force – not by fitting weapons to the troop-carriers, as the added weight would have reduced the number of men they could carry, but by providing 'gunship' escorts whose sole task was to keep down the heads of the waiting enemy.

Most suitable candidate for the new role was the Bell UH-1A Iroquois, known usually as the 'Huey' since it went into production with the original designation HU-1. Thirteen of these aircraft were each fitted with a pair of 0·30 in machineguns and two pods containing a total of 16 2·75 in air-to-ground rockets, mounted on the landing gear skids to each side of the cabin and fired by a crewman in the open doorway. Casualties among assault parties soon fell dramatically, and some of the larger troop-carriers later began to acquire their own defensive armament.

So successful was the 'Huey gunship' that the US Army

CH-46 Sea Knight transport helicopter armed with a heavy gun for self defence

HueyCobra attack helicopter in action against an enemy convoy of trucks and armoured vehicles

ordered from its makers, the Bell Helicopter Company, a specially designed attack version. To save time and cost, and to take advantage of well-proven components, Bell retained the basic power plant and rotor system of the 'Huey' and simply fitted a completely new fuselage. This is only 38 in (96·5 cm) wide, making it a difficult target to hit during a head-on attack.

Instead of carrying up to 14 troops or six stretcher patients, the new aircraft, designated AH-1G HueyCobra, has only two crewmen, one behind the other. The copilot-gunner sits in front above a rotatable turret housing two multi-barrel machine-guns (Miniguns) or two 40 mm grenade launchers, or one of each. Behind him, on a raised seat that provides a fine field of vision, is the pilot, who is normally responsible for weapons carried under the Cobra's small stub-wings. On the AH-1G these usually consist of four pods containing 76 rockets, two more Miniguns, a 20 mm gun pack or a mixture of these weapons.

The Cobra entered service in Vietnam in 1967, proving so effective that the US Army eventually ordered more than one thousand. When TOW wire-guided anti-tank missiles were developed for air-launching, these were added to the aircraft's armament, the new version being known as the AH-1Q TOW/Cobra. Only a handful of these missile-armed models were available in time to be sent to Vietnam. In two months they launched 77 TOWs, scoring 62 hits on small targets and destroying 39 armoured vehicles, trucks and howitzers. None of the helicopters was hit by hostile fire.

So, by mid-1972, the 'chopper' had given new meaning to its nickname. The agile HueyCobra could reach a battle area in about half the time taken by a UH-1 Iroquois. It had been dived at nearly 250 mph (400 km/h) during tests and carried sufficient fuel to remain in the target area for about three times as long as a UH-1. Its low profile enabled it to stay under cover until enemy vehicles approached; then it could pop up speedily, fire its weapons and race home at treetop height.

Once the HueyCobra had demonstrated the potential of a heavily armed and armoured attack and escort helicopter, other manufacturers were quick to get in on the act. First design from another company to enter service, in 1973–74, was the formidable Soviet Mil Mi-24, known to NATO as 'Hind'. This combines to a degree the capabilities of the American UH-1 Iroquois and AH-1 TOW/Cobra, being a powerfully armed transport for a squad of eight assault troops.

Russia stationed its early Mi-24s on each flank of the Warsaw Treaty ground forces confronting NATO in Europe. If confrontation ever escalated into something more serious, the aircraft would stream over the border, fast and low, dispersing the opposition with nose machine-guns and the four large rocket packs that each carries under its stub-wings. In the drop-zone, armoured forces could be attacked with four anti-tank guided missiles mounted on the wingtips, before the Mi-24s disembarked their tough, highly trained occupants and roared back to base for more.

Experience in Vietnam showed that when the temperature

The Soviet Mil Mi-24 combines transport and attack roles

Hughes YAH-64 Advanced Attack Helicopter — one of the types under evaluation as a successor to the HueyCobra

was high the TOW/Cobra did not have sufficient engine power to carry the planned load of eight missiles. It achieved impressive successes with smaller numbers, but Bell began work on a new version, the AH-1S, with a more powerful engine. Meanwhile, the US Army ordered prototypes of two new Advanced Attack Helicopters (AAH) from the Bell and Hughes companies for competitive evaluation.

Although similar to the Cobra in configuration, Bell's YAH-63 is much heavier, with two 1,500 hp engines instead of the earlier aircraft's single 1,100 hp engine. Like its competitor, the Hughes YAH-64, it is a two-seater armed with a turret-mounted 30 mm gun, eight TOW missiles and two pods of rockets. Use of infra-red and other equipment will enable the AAHs to operate by night or day. To facilitate storage or delivery by transport aircraft, the YAH-64 has removable wings, a collapsible undercarriage and a folding tail which greatly reduces its overall dimensions.

Kamov Ka-25 operating from the Russian Navy's anti-submarine helicopter carrier *Moskva*

Until helicopters could carry a large enough load for more aggressive duties, they served in small numbers at sea for carrying personnel between ships or ship-to-shore, and flying 'plane guard' to pick up quickly the crew of any fixed-wing aircraft unfortunate enough to end up in the sea during normal carrier operations – a task in which they replaced destroyers, at great saving in cost and speed of rescue.

By the mid-fifties, helicopters were, at least nominally, submarine hunter-killers. One 'chopper' normally carried search gear, including a sonar device which could be lowered into the water at the end of a cable to 'listen' for a submerged submarine while the aircraft hovered over the sea. A second aircraft carried torpedoes of a type that would home on the sound of any submarine detected. During operations by these helicopters, a variety of new equipment was evolved to improve the effectiveness of their anti-submarine operations, by day and night, in all weathers. The Sikorsky company introduced on the HSS-1 automatic stabilization to overcome the instability that had been a bugbear of helicopter flying. Ryan produced a highly accurate and self-contained Doppler radar navigation system for the same aircraft, which could be pre-set to hover automatically at a chosen height over any pre-selected point. Rockets, depth charges and air-to-surface missiles were added to armament options. Search radar and dipping sonar were supplemented on Soviet helicopters by a towed magnetic anomaly detector, at the end of a long cable, to locate the metallic mass of a submerged submarine.

Britain's Royal Navy ordered from the Westland company a version of the HSS-1, known as the Wessex, with turbine engines. So started a whole new chapter in the history of the military helicopter, which gained immensely in performance and efficiency from that time. It was possible to combine the hunter and killer roles in new designs, like the twin-turbine Sikorsky Sea King, and helicopters became standard anti-submarine types in all the major navies of the world, flying from small platforms on convoy escort ships as well as from aircraft carriers.

The Royal Navy's Sea King carries its search radar in a fuselage hump

Israeli Magister armed trainer *v* Arab tank in June 1967

TRAINERS WITH TEETH

During the Six-Day War in the Middle East in June 1967, a number of Arab tank crews suffered the indignity of being put out of action by converted training aircraft. The idea of pressing into combat service every aeroplane capable of carrying weapons at a time of national emergency was by no means new. As long ago as January 1918, the British Royal Flying Corps had decided to adapt more than 200 D.H.6 trainers to carry a single 100 lb (45 kg) bomb, so that they could join in the life-and-death struggle against German U-boats in the waters around the United Kingdom, which posed such a threat to Allied shipping.

The D.H.6 was neither handsome nor a high performer. Its square-cut biplane wings were said to be 'made by the mile

and bought by the yard'. Nicknames ranged from 'The Clutching Hand', due to its heavily cambered wings, to 'The Flying Coffin', because of its long, open cockpit for two. When carrying a bomb it could lift only the pilot and had a maximum speed of less than 75 mph (120 km/h); but it operated in all but the worst weather, and U-boat commanders preferred to keep their periscopes down, and their submarines submerged and harmless, in areas known to be patrolled by D.H.6s.

Even in the Second World War, Tiger Moth biplane trainers were fitted hastily with racks for small bombs when the invasion of Britain appeared imminent in 1940. But this was another desperate attempt to make use of anything that would fly, however unsuitable for the task. The Magister jet trainers operated as strike aircraft by the Israelis in 1967 were very different.

Designed in France, the graceful little Magister had two

880 lb (400 kg) thrust turbojet engines and was much faster than any of the fighters once used in the Battle of Britain. Armament included two machine-guns and underwing racks for two 110 lb (50 kg) bombs, air-to-ground missiles, or rocket packs. So, although designed as the world's first jet basic trainer in the early 'fifties, it had clear potential as a low-cost, easy-to-fly, light attack aircraft from the start.

One of the biggest problems that confronted United Nations forces in Korea in 1950 stemmed from the enemy's skill at concealment on the ground. Pilots in high-speed fighters often flew directly over infiltrating enemy patrols and combat units without suspecting that they were there, and the situation did not improve until the USAF brought in veteran North American T-6 (Harvard) piston-engined trainers for what became known as Mosquito missions. Carrying trained army observers, these old aircraft flew from front-line airstrips to act as 'spotters' for the UN ground forces. If they caught sight of the enemy, they dived to mark his position with smoke rockets as a warning to friendly troops and a guide for the fighter-bombers they called in by radio to deal with the threat.

Such operations in Korea and elsewhere introduced the new term 'counter-insurgency' (COIN) into the military airman's vocabulary. It covered any mission flown against invading bands of guerrillas, terrorists and similar ground forces that were lightly equipped but well skilled in moving unobserved through difficult terrain and living off the land. Obsolete trainers like the T-6 and its successor, the T-28, proved ideal for seeking out the insurgents, and could themselves be fitted with guns, bombs, rockets and armour plate to become low-cost attack aircraft. In Vietnam, T-28s performed such outstanding service against the Vietcong in areas where there were no heavy anti-aircraft defences that the USAF and Vietnamese Air Force eagerly snapped up hundreds of retired US Navy Skyraider piston-engined attack aircraft as even more formidable COIN types, able to carry huge loads of bombs and rockets. Today, such aircraft – no longer suitable for their original role – operate with air forces throughout Africa, Asia and South America, wherever there is a threat to the security or stability

T-28 trainer converted for COIN operations in Vietnam

Strikemaster, an attack version of the Jet Provost trainer

of any nation through the action of dissident or irregular forces, which may be trained and armed by other nations.

Conversion of ancient piston-engined aircraft for COIN operations could only be a temporary, low-cost expedient. The supply of such types was limited, they could not be expected to remain airworthy for ever, and the availability to insurgents of lightweight, shoulder-fired, homing anti-aircraft missiles, like the Soviet SA-7, made the slower aircraft increasingly vulnerable. On the other hand, it was clear to many small nations that they could not afford both a first-class, regular air force and a second air force equipped with new counter-insurgency aircraft to deal with border incidents and bands of well-armed terrorists.

The answer (as already mentioned on pages 56–57) was a modern mini-jet that could spend most of its life as a primary trainer but be easily adaptable for ground attack duties whenever the need arose. Little extra work or cost is involved in making an aircraft suitable for such dual roles. A modern basic trainer has to be capable of 'all-through' instruction, from the pupil's first day at the controls to when he is ready for advanced training in operational techniques. It is usually designed to carry small practice bombs and rockets, plus the necessary gunsights and other equipment. By making the wing structure and undercarriage a little stronger than they would need to be for such work, it is simple to make provision for heavier underwing weapon loads when the aircraft is flown in single-seat, light attack form.

Almost all basic trainers used by world air forces have this dual capability, including the British Jet Provost, American T-37, French Magister, Swedish Saab-105, Italian Aermacchi MB 326, Yugoslav Galeb, Polish Iskra and Czechoslovakian L-39 Albatros. In some cases, too, the manufacturers offer a

Cessna's A-37 is a heavily armed attack aircraft based on the T-37 trainer

specialized version with a more powerful engine, higher performance and greater load-carrying ability that make it primarily an inexpensive combat aircraft. A good example is the Strikemaster, evolved from the Jet Provost.

Italy's Aermacchi MB 326 has proved to be one of the most successful dual-role jet trainer/attack designs yet put on the market. The original prototype, first flown on 10 December 1957, was a two-seat basic trainer with a British Viper 8 turbojet engine of only 1,750 lb (794 kg) thrust. It went into production for the air forces of Italy and Australia with a more powerful engine, the 2,500 lb (1,134 kg) thrust Viper 11. Simultaneously, other air forces worldwide became interested in dual-role attack/trainer versions and there was soon a whole family of variants of the same basic design.

A typical example is the MB 326GB/GC, a 539 mph (867 km/h) dual-role aircraft with a 3,410 lb (1,547 kg) thrust Viper 20, which can carry nearly two tons of rockets, bombs, gun packs, missiles, reconnaissance pods or other stores under its wings. From it, Aermacchi evolved the single-seat MB 326K with a 4,000 lb (1,814 kg) thrust Viper, extra fuel, heavier weapon load and provision for cockpit armour. No makeshift, the K can be fitted with a full range of modern combat electronics and equipment, including Doppler navigation radar, a laser rangefinder and a bombing computer. The MB 326L is similar, but with two seats instead of one for training duties.

Nor is this the final production model, for the prototype of a redesigned two-seat version known as the MB 339 is scheduled to fly in 1976, nearly 19 years after the first MB 326. The basic airframe and power plant are like those of the single-seat 326K, but the forward fuselage now seats the instructor, in the rear seat, higher than the pupil, giving him a much improved view. Armament is also heavier, with provision for a 30 mm gun in a pod under the fuselage. So, by continuous refinement, a basically sound design has remained in production for two decades, offering two aircraft for the price of one at far lower total programme cost than if each major development stage had required a completely new type.

The many variants of the Aermacchi MB 326 include the MB 326GB attack aircraft (*top*) and the MB 326H basic trainer

ASSAULT TRANSPORTS

Anyone who envisages a military transport as simply an airliner with a different paint-scheme has much to learn. For half a century, the crews of such aircraft have had to be prepared to fly into trouble spots anywhere in the world, at a moment's notice. During the winter of 1928–29, for example, RAF crews had to fly their primitive Victoria biplanes over 10,000 ft (3,050 m) mountain ranges, in some of the worst weather on record, to snatch 586 people – including the King of Afghanistan – from under the guns of a rebel army besieging Kabul. The courage and sacrifice of Luftwaffe crews who flew paratroops to Crete in 1941, and of RAF crews who carried men and towed gliders to Arnhem in 1944, contributed some of the proudest chapters in military history. After the Second World War, unarmed transports prevented an even more terrible war by keeping a city of more than two million people alive, by air supply, during the Berlin Air Lift of 1948–49. Fifty-one

Bearing no identifying insignia, a Courier lands in a small clearing in the mountains

Paratroops dropping from an An-12 of the Soviet Air Force during a military exercise

airmen died in 17 serious accidents in an operation that should never have been necessary.

The Berlin Air Lift made newspaper headlines for over a year; some tactical transport operations, flown continuously for many years and still taking place, are never publicised. Typical are missions flown in parts of South America, and elsewhere, by Helio U-10D Courier six-seat STOL transports. Able to land and take off in ridiculously small spaces, these spindly machines come and go stealthily – sometimes dropping security forces in remote areas to deal with bands of intruders, at other times engaging in exploits that make James Bond stories seem tame by comparison.

A Courier, flown often without insignia, has an engine of only 295 hp and a top speed of 167 mph (269 km/h). At the other extreme are assault transports like Russia's 100-passenger four-turboprop Antonov An-12 and its successor, the mighty four-turbofan Ilyushin Il-76, which can carry a 40-tonne load for 3,100 miles (5,000 km) at 528 mph (850 km/h).

Gliders were used to deliver highly trained airborne troops to many key battle areas in the Second World War. Quiet and expendable, they could be released over areas completely lacking in airfields for powered transport aircraft. It was considered that they could put their occupants down more precisely in the correct place, and in better organized, more concentrated groups, than by a drop of parachute troops.

Casualties were high as the gliders often came down in darkness, in small, tree-lined fields and under the noses of the enemy. Today, to the relief of everyone concerned, gliders have been replaced by helicopters. The quietness of a glider drop has gone; but the 'choppers' can come into their drop-zone low and fast, putting down many more troops than were carried by gliders, safely and in the right place.

Great progress has been made in the quarter-century since helicopters first proved themselves as front-line transports in Korea. The US Army's CH-47 Chinook can haul a 10-ton payload over short distances at speeds up to 140 mph (225 km/h). Its stability and control are so good that it was often hovered with its open tail-ramp against a hilltop in Vietnam, so that its load of up to 44 troops, supplies, guns or vehicles could be disembarked in places where even a helicopter could not find sufficient space to land. Nor was the official maximum load figure taken too seriously. On one occasion, a Chinook evacuated 147 refugees and their possessions on a single flight.

In addition to their go-anywhere capability, helicopters offer other advantages over fixed-wing transports in a combat area. Loads which are too big to go inside their cabin, or which have to be delivered to a place where touchdown is impossible, can be hauled in a sling or at the end of a cable under the fuselage. Casualties can be picked up almost anywhere by ambulance helicopters, and airmen who have come down in enemy territory or at sea can be hoisted aboard while the helicopter hovers – a technique that has already saved countless thousands of lives.

With its tail against a ridge, a Chinook disembarks troops

Extracting a load by drag-chute from a low-flying C-130 Hercules

Parachuting of men, equipment and supplies into combat areas remains an important duty of tactical air transport squadrons, enabling them to deliver heavy loads in places completely lacking in airfields. Helicopters are too limited in speed and range for use on anything but local operations. However, increasing emphasis has been placed in recent years on the development of large-capacity, fixed-wing transports which can be operated into small, rough landing areas and be unloaded and loaded very quickly. This has led, inevitably, to aircraft with nose and tail loading doors. In most cases the rear doors can be opened in flight, and a ramp lowered partially, to permit items as large as guns and armoured vehicles to be dropped by parachute to troops on the ground.

This is not so easy as it sounds. Loads have to be stowed carefully in an aeroplane to maintain a balance around the

centre of gravity. The effect of trundling a large vehicle from one end of the cabin to the other and pushing it out of a hole near the tail, without offsetting the change in 'trim', is easy to imagine. The results of a heavy landing for the parachuted load could also be serious, which explains the need for clusters of large parachutes and inflatable airbags to cushion the touch-down of some heavy items. Even more spectacular is the Soviet use of retro-rockets which fire automatically when the load is within a few feet of the ground to slow its descent at the last moment.

Most paradrops are made from hundreds or thousands of feet above the ground, requiring great skill in allowing for wind speed and consequent drift. In contrast, one technique used by the crews of C-130 Hercules transports involves flying low over the drop-zone with the rear ramp down. At the right moment a parachute is popped to tug the load out of the rear of the cabin and deposit it on the ground a few feet beneath the aircraft. Although less rough than it sounds, it is not a method recommended for eggs or electronics!

Lockheed's C-130 Hercules has proved such an efficient and successful transport that its eventual replacement will have to be something very special. The time for that replacement is still some years away. In fact, with more than 1,400 Hercules already delivered in dozens of different versions, the rate of production had to be doubled to six a month in 1974–75 to keep pace with orders.

To allow plenty of time for development of an Advanced Medium STOL Transport (AMST) embodying the latest design concepts and aerodynamic advances, the USAF announced its future requirement to nine of America's leading aircraft manufacturers in 1972. In November it ordered two prototypes of Boeing's design, which it designated YC-14, and two of the McDonnell Douglas design, which became the YC-15.

As in the case of the YF-16 and YF-17 lightweight fighters (pages 44–45) these two aircraft, designed to the same specification, proved to be very different in configuration. Both are high-wing monoplanes with wide-bodied fuselage, rear loading ramp and a T-tail but, whereas the YC-15 is of fairly conventional layout, with four Pratt & Whitney JT8D-17 turbofans (each 16,000 lb, 7,257 kg thrust), the YC-14 has only two very powerful General Electric CF6-50Ds (each 51,000 lb, 23,133 kg thrust) mounted above and forward of the wing roots. This looks strange, but enables the jet exhaust to pass over the top of the wings and then down over special Coanda-type flaps which give a huge increase in lift during take-off and landing. Boeing claims that this 'powered lift' idea will enable the YC-14 to lift a 27,000 lb (12,247 kg) payload out of rough airfields no more than 2,000 ft (610 m) long.

McDonnell Douglas claims a precisely similar performance for the YC-15, which emphasises that the design is less orthodox than it appears to be. In fact, both aircraft make use of the revolutionary 'supercritical' low-drag, thick wing section evolved in recent years by NASA. The YC-15 has its four engines mounted in such a way that their exhaust flows back under the wings, where a part is deflected by the flaps downward and the rest passes between the flaps via wide slots and continues down the other side, creating about double the lift

Boeing YC-14. The unique positioning of the two big turbofans enables their exhaust gases to be passed back over the wings and flaps, greatly increasing lift during take-off and landing

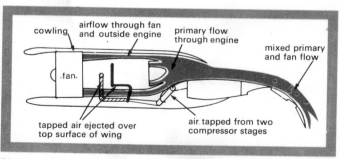

Diagram of airflow over the YC-14's wing at take-off. By tapping air from two places in the compressor casing and ejecting it just behind the wing leading-edge, airflow can be made to 'cling' to the wing over the entire span

The McDonnell Douglas YC-15 appears quite conventional, but has a very advanced high-lift wing and 'flap blowing' system

of a conventional design. As well as permitting the aircraft to operate from 2,000 ft strips, this makes possible approach and steep descent speeds as low as 98 mph (158 km/h).

The YC-15's fuselage contains 67 per cent more cargo space than the USAF's largest current medium transport, enabling it to carry up to 40 troops and six pallets of cargo simultaneously, containers up to 9 ft (2·7 m) high or eight army Jeeps in two rows of four. Weapons that can be accommodated include standard self-propelled artillery such as the 8 in (203 mm) howitzer and 175 mm gun, M48 Chaparral and M163 Vulcan air defence vehicles, and construction equipment like the scoop loader or 5-ton dump truck.

As a STOL transport, the YC-15 will carry its nominal 27,000 lb payload for a distance of 460 miles (740 km) and return without refuelling. Alternatively, when conventional

airfield runways can be used, it will carry a 62,000 lb (28,120 kg) load over the same radius. If it becomes available one day for commercial use, operators will appreciate the fact that its engines are of the same basic type as those which power the DC-9, Boeing 727 and Boeing 737 airliners. Its entire cockpit enclosure is identical with that of the DC-10 commercial transport, with two additional downward-viewing windows to provide improved visibility during operations into short airstrips in rugged terrain.

Civil-operated YC-15s would be able to use secondary airports located in or near population centres, and would have a range of about 2,000 miles (3,220 km) carrying 150 passengers in a fuselage of the present size or 200 in 'stretched' form. By transferring the advanced design features to a completely new STOL airliner, McDonnell Douglas believes it could produce a commercial transport as significant in flying history as the old DC-3 Dakota or Boeing 747 'Jumbo'.

A UN peace-keeping force disembarks at a trouble spot, having been airlifted complete with all its equipment

STRATEGIC TRANSPORTS

These are the biggest military aircraft of all, some of them far exceeding the size and weight of even the mightiest bombers. Unlike tactical transports, they seldom become involved in combat operations although an enemy would certainly try to destroy them if he were able to do so, as the men and material they carry are often vital to the continued effectiveness of day-to-day operations in the field.

Strategic transports are responsible for the routine support of a nation's armed forces wherever they may be and whatever they are doing. Supplies and equipment must be ferried to overseas garrisons. Men due for transfer or leave must be flown out, complete perhaps with families and possessions. Replacements must be brought in and provision made for the speedy evacuation of anyone who needs to dash home for

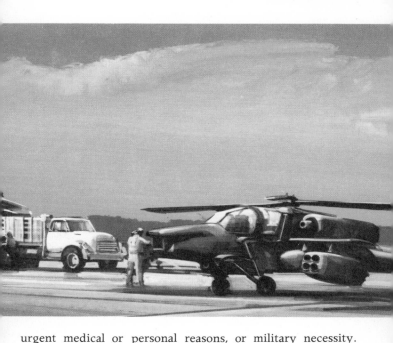

urgent medical or personal reasons, or military necessity.

No single type of aircraft could perform all these tasks efficiently and economically. Only the very largest transport aircraft can accommodate an army main battle tank or missile transporter/erector/launcher. A smaller cabin, fitted out with comfortable bunks, oxygen and a full range of medical equipment, is preferable for air ambulance flights that must sometimes carry men and women quickly across the world. A 200-seat passenger jet sent to collect ten men from a tiny island base would be as impractical as despatching a ten-seater to fly the band of the Royal Marines to an official engagement in Germany.

It is difficult to suggest the total size of the world's military strategic air transport forces, as aircraft like the Hercules are often used for both tactical and strategic duties. The USAF has about 1,200 fixed-wing transports of all types; the Soviet Air Force has 1,500, with the world's biggest airline, Aeroflot, as a reserve. By comparison, the RAF retains only 57 fixed-wing transports, the majority of them being C-130 Hercules;

The famous C-47 (DC-3) troop transport of the Second World War looks tiny by comparison with a giant C-5A Galaxy

however, even such a modest fleet can perform an immense amount of work in a year, including relief operations in areas hit by natural disasters such as floods, drought or earthquake.

One of the more colourful officers of America's Civil War era, General Nathan Bedford Forrest, had a favourite saying, that the key to victory in war was to 'Git thar fustest with the mostest'. The designers of modern military air transports do their best to make this possible – none more so than the Lockheed team which was responsible for the C-5A Galaxy. In terms of overall dimensions, rather than take-off weight, the Galaxy is the largest aeroplane in service. It can carry its maximum payload of 220,967 lb (100,228 kg) for 3,749 miles (6,033 km) without even refuelling in flight. Normally, it is

operated as a freighter, but there are 75 troop seats on the upper deck, behind the flight crew compartments, with provision for carrying 270 more troops on the main deck, if required. Capacity is, therefore, much the same as that of a commercial Boeing 747 airliner, which can carry as many passengers across the Atlantic in a year as four ocean liners the size of the old *Queen Mary*. This helps to underline the vast work capacity of the USAF's Military Airlift Command, whose fleet includes nearly 80 Galaxies.

To save time on the ground, the whole nose of the Galaxy is built to hinge upward like the vizor of a medieval knight's helmet, giving access to the full 19 ft (5·8 m) width of the 34,795 cu ft (985 m³) main hold. The undercarriage can be made to 'kneel' so that vehicles can drive inside up a short ramp. Simultaneously, other loading or unloading can be done via the customary rear loading ramp. Few items of military equipment are too bulky to be 'swallowed'. During the

Vietnam War, loads such as two M-48 Army tanks, each weighing 99,000 lb (45,000 kg), or three CH-47 Chinook helicopters, were airlifted across the Pacific by individual aircraft at a cruising speed well above 500 mph (800 km/h).

There is probably no other aircraft in the world with a main deck so easily accessible as that of the Galaxy, and designers and operators show great ingenuity in their effort to make the best possible use of types which lack its huge nose door and ability to 'kneel'. More and more freight is pre-packed in standard containers to fill every inch of available cabin space. Inside the cabin, the containers or freight pallets glide smoothly and easily over rollers and castors set in the floor. In some aircraft the rollers are powered, so that loads weighing many tons can be moved about the cabin by one or two men at a control panel. Winches on the floor and gantries on the roof help to move loads in other aircraft. Conversion from freighter to passenger transport often involves no more than putting aboard pallets of seats, complete with galley and toilet units, instead of freight containers or pallets.

Sometimes, what appear to be strategic transports are really special-purpose military aircraft designed for the most important military tasks of all. This is certainly true of the E-4B. From a distance it looks little different from any other Boeing 747, except for the insignia which proclaims proudly 'United States of America' instead of the name of an airline. Inside, however, the equipment is different from that of aircraft in service with any commercial operator in the world.

The E-4B is an Advanced Airborne National Command Post (AABNCP). This means that at least one of the planned fleet of seven would be in the air every second of every day during a period when there was the possibility of an attack on the USA by a foreign power. Such an attack, if carried out with nuclear

Top left Loading and unloading a Galaxy is made easy by raising the vizor nose and 'kneeling' the undercarriage
Top right The main deck of a Boeing 747 is 16 ft (4·90 m) above ground level, but the upward-hinged nose door and a powered conveyor system in the cabin enable two men to load 120 tons in 30 minutes
Bottom To speed loading in the field, the cabin floor of the C-130 Hercules is at the same height above the ground as the average truck bed

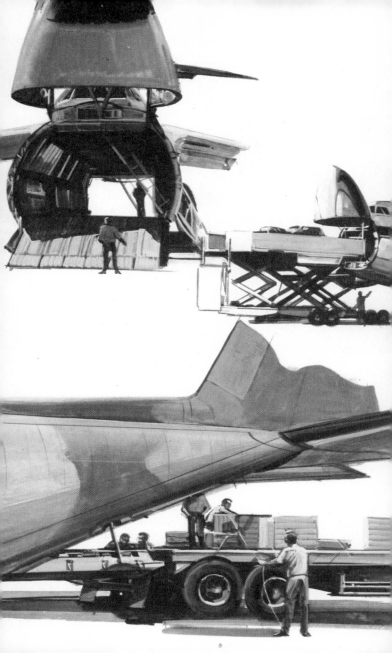

The command centre of an Airborne Command Post, equipped to control and direct the entire US war effort in the event of a nuclear attack

missiles, might knock out all the regular channels of command on the ground. The E-4B would then take over, to command and control Strategic Air Command's (SAC's) huge force of bombers and ICBMs that would be at instant readiness to launch an overwhelming counter-attack.

Replacing earlier EC-135s, based on the Boeing 707, the E-4Bs can carry an expanded battle staff in far greater comfort, including even the President at a time of extreme emergency. Telephone calls and radio messages that would normally go to the White House, the Pentagon, SAC Headquarters or other command centres would be passed directly to the E-4B via satellite links. Decisions made and buttons pressed in flight would then unleash the forces of destruction as efficiently as any normal command chain on the ground. Even the crews of

US Navy submarines, on station in the far oceans of the world, would know if the time had come to fire their Polaris and Poseidon missiles.

If this ever happened, the nuclear deterrent would have failed and much of mankind would be doomed. Existence of aircraft like the E-4B, able to survive an initial surprise attack because they are airborne, is another good reason why the deterrent will not fail.

The KC-135 is another key military aircraft which had its origin in a jet airliner. It is, in fact, so vital to the operational capability of the USAF that it was ordered into production in October 1954, less than three months after Boeing flew its original prototype jet transport and nine months before the company received approval to build the commercial 707 for airline service.

About ten years had passed since the RAF had planned to

F-111 swing-wing fighter refuelling from a KC-135 tanker

add the wartime Bomber Command's might to that of US forces attacking Japan by using flight refuelling to give its aircraft the necessary range. SAC was now equipped with fuel-thirsty jets and it had long been clear that only the use of flight refuelling could make America's nuclear deterrent policy effective, by enabling the big jet bombers to attack any target in the world.

The British technique required the pilot of the 'receiver' to start the fuel transfer by ramming a probe on his aircraft into a conical drogue at the end of a flexible hose trailed by the tanker. The US system, first fitted to old piston-engined Superfortress bombers, made a crewman in the tanker responsible for contact by requiring him to 'fly' the end of a rigid boom into a socket on the receiver.

Tests with a 'flying boom' on the prototype of the Boeing 707 showed that a refined production version of this jet aircraft could increase the effectiveness of the whole concept by

taking off with no less than 25,980 gallons (118,100 litres) of fuel in its tanks, any amount of which could be transferred to another aircraft at a rate of 830 gallons (3,780 litres) a minute. A total of 732 of the production KC-135A tankers were delivered eventually to the USAF. The US Navy preferred the British 'probe and drogue' technique, variations of which were soon adopted also by the RAF and the French and Soviet Air Forces. Before long, it became routine for most types of bomber, fighter, attack, reconnaissance, and transport aircraft, and even large helicopters, to top up their tanks by rendezvousing with one or more tankers during long flights.

In addition to 732 KC-135A jet tankers, Boeing built for the USAF 76 other military adaptations of the 707 airliner. Some were straightforward transports; others were fitted with cameras for reconnaissance and mapping. As they were replaced in their original roles, many were converted for new tasks. Often, these were the kind of jobs that receive little

Boeing E-3A AWACS, with radar so efficient that it will pick out
fast, low-flying aircraft against any degree of ground 'clutter'

publicity, like tracking, identifying and photographing warheads of Soviet test missiles as they re-enter the atmosphere
over the Pacific, or flying around the borders of certain
countries, outside the national airspace, using sensors to probe
the secrets of their defences (see page 116).

Modification for such missions gave the basic C-135
aircraft strange shapes and difficult-to-recognize designations
such as NKC-135A and KC-135R. But no variant had a stranger
appearance than the two experimental EC-137Ds converted
from Boeing 707s and first flown in 1972. They were not the
first aircraft to carry above their fuselage a saucer-shape
radome which rotated slowly in flight to locate any aircraft
flying within its long-range scan. The US Navy had operated
E-2 Hawkeyes with a similar radar from its aircraft carriers
for some years, and the Russians had adapted their big Tu-114

four-turboprop airliner into the military Tu-126, with 36 ft (11 m) diameter radome of the same saucer shape.

Similar shape does not, however, imply equal capability. Tests soon showed that the EC-137Ds were the first aircraft of their kind able to pinpoint low-flying raiders over any kind of terrain, ashore or at sea, whereas the Tu-126 (known to NATO as 'Moss') is fully effective only over water. After several years of development, the Boeing aircraft was put into production for the USAF as the E-3A AWACS (Airborne Warning And Control System). The acronym reflects the fact that it not only locates attackers, flying at any height, but can direct fighters to intercept them. It can, in fact, direct the entire friendly air forces in the area where it operates, including strike, defence, airlift, reconnaissance, and close support squadrons. Its crew of 17 includes 13 AWACS specialists.

Russia's counterpart, the Tupolev Tu-126, based on the familiar Tu-114 four-turboprop long-range airliner

MARITIME RECONNAISSANCE

During two World Wars the biggest threat to Britain's survival came from German U-boat operations, which endangered the nation's vital sea supply routes. It is no coincidence that both America and Russia continue to operate huge submarine fleets, and it is more important than ever to be able to keep track of the movements of such craft and to destroy them now that many carry nuclear missiles.

Maritime reconnaissance (MR) and attack remain, therefore, two of the major responsibilities of the air forces of nations bordering oceans and seas. Up to the Second World War, this involved mainly the deployment of multi-engined flying-boats which were believed to be safer than landplanes for overwater operation. Such misapprehensions vanished long ago, helped by the higher performance and simpler, more

While one PS-1 searches for a submarine with its underwater sonar, another takes off for a practice attack on the 'enemy' craft

economical operation of landplanes. It was, therefore, surprising to learn in the mid-sixties that Japan intended to develop a new, large, STOL, anti-submarine flying-boat for service with its Maritime Self-Defence Force (JMSDF).

The prototype of the Shin Meiwa PS-1 flew on 5 October 1967, and proved outstanding from the start. In addition to the full range of equipment carried by the average shore-based MR aircraft, it has a special sonar which it can dip deep into the sea during repeated landings and take-offs, giving it a search capability matched only by a hovering helicopter. Four 3,060 hp turboprops provide a maximum speed of 340 mph (547 km/h) and normal range of 1,347 miles (2,168 km). Any hostile submarine or surface ship located can be attacked with four homing torpedoes carried in underwing pods, six 5 in rockets and four 330 lb (150 kg) anti-submarine bombs.

The JMSDF has a squadron of PS-1s fully operational, plus a small number of PS-1 Mod amphibious models for search and

rescue. A 69-passenger transport version is under consideration, and a water bomber version for attacking forest fires is under test.

The Shin Meiwa PS-1 flying-boat is no lightweight. It spans 108 ft 8¾ in (33·14 m), has a take-off weight of 94,800 lb (43,000 kg) and carries a crew of ten. But not all MR aircraft are so large or carry such complex equipment; in some places the ships that must be located and dealt with are not nuclear submarines, but Chinese junks crewed by would-be smugglers. There is little point in using a £3½ million flying-boat to search for such a boat when a 160 mph (260 km/h) armed transport like the little Britten-Norman Defender can do an equally good job at a hundredth of the initial purchase price.

It would be difficult to imagine a more simple, practical, military general-purpose aircraft than the Defender. It is an adaptation of the Islander commercial transport, of which more than 600 have been sold to civilian operators, with a pair of well-proven 300 hp Lycoming piston-engines and a fixed tricycle undercarriage.

Typical of places that have bought Defenders is Hong Kong, where the Royal Hong Kong Auxiliary Air Force has just six aircraft and 100 part-time personnel of Chinese, European, Australian and African nationality. Rescue and air ambulance missions take up much of its time, but excitement comes through incidents such as smuggling encounters, when the Defender mounts light weapons under its wings in case of trouble. Alternative weapon loads available for the aircraft include twin machine-gun packs, 250 lb or 500 lb bombs, rocket packs, wire-guided missiles and anti-personnel grenades. On less aggressive missions, the aircraft can carry a pilot and nine passengers, three stretcher cases and two attendants, or a cabin-full of freight. The same nose radar that locates a smuggler's boat, or helps the pilot to avoid bad weather, can also be of major help when searching for a wreck or survivors during air-sea rescue missions – a multi-role capability that makes this inexpensive aircraft ideal for tiny air forces.

When the first high-speed, deep-diving nuclear-powered

A Defender escorts into harbour a junk suspected of smuggling

A 'pattern' of sonobuoys being dropped from an Orion

submarines entered service, it was reckoned that crews of anti-submarine aircraft had a virtually impossible task. If they knew that the ship they were seeking was in a particular, not-too-large volume of ocean, they had a reasonable chance of locating it. But if they had to hunt for a submarine – *any* submarine – anywhere in the waters that cover 70·8 per cent of the Earth's surface, it would clearly be easier to find the proverbial needle in a haystack.

As with all military situations involving a conflict between offence and defence, this will be resolved eventually. The favourite theory is that, one day, satellites will be able to probe under the water to locate precisely the position and depth of every submarine at sea. Destruction in a missile age should then be easy.

Meanwhile, the new search equipment and weapons being evolved continuously for MR aircraft are enhancing their chance of success year by year. The most widely used type in the mid-seventies is the four-turboprop Lockheed P-3 Orion supplied to the US Navy, Australia, Iran, New Zealand, Norway and Spain. Its search equipment includes a nose radar, tail MAD 'sting' which detects anything metallic below the aircraft, an ECM direction finder which fixes the position of electronic emissions from a submarine, a searchlight, low light level TV for surface search, a device which can tell when a submarine has passed through a stretch of water by detecting a small increase in water temperature, underwater sound signal transmitters and sonobuoys. Dropped in 'patterns', these last two devices detect a submerged submarine by emitting sound and sonar signals respectively, which are reflected back from the submarine, picked up and fed into a computer which converts them into bearings and distances.

The latest P-3C Orion can carry 20,000 lb (9,070 kg) of expendable stores, a typical load including six 2,000 lb mines under the wings, 87 sonobuoys inside chutes in the rear fuselage, and two depth bombs and four homing torpedoes in the weapon bay. It can remain on patrol for three hours after flying 1,550 miles (2,500 km) to a search area.

The MR aircraft of the Soviet Union, which are sent out over the oceans of the world to keep track of NATO fleet movements,

An Orion attacks with underwing rockets a submarine that it has surprised on the surface

are mostly adaptations of strategic bombers. For years the most numerous have been versions of the Tupolev twin-jet Tu-16 and four-turboprop Tu-95, known to NATO as 'Badger' and 'Bear' respectively, with smaller numbers of four-jet Myasishchev M-4s (NATO 'Bison'). They were joined in about 1970 by the first Ilyushin Il-38s (NATO 'May'), evolved from the Il-18 airliner and similar in size to the American P-3 Orion. In the mid-seventies a far more formidable type began to be seen, in the form of a maritime version of the Tupolev 'Backfire' supersonic swing-wing bomber.

Some versions of the Tupolev bombers carry air-to-surface missiles for use against surface ships. Others are equipped with powerful radars, underwing electronic intelligence-gathering pods and assorted search, reconnaissance and 'spying' devices. Of particular interest are the 'Bear-D' and 'Bear-F' versions of the Tu-95, each of which has a huge radome under its centre fuselage. The idea is that in wartime the 'Bears' would track down enemy ships and radio their precise position to Soviet missile-armed naval vessels many miles away. The latter would then launch their missiles, which would be tracked in

Soviet Tu-95 ('Bear-D') maritime reconnaissance and missile guidance aircraft

A Tu-16 ('Badger') MR aircraft of the Soviet Northern Fleet at its snow-covered base

flight by the 'Bears' while continuing to keep the targets under observation. Any necessary course corrections could be passed to the missile controllers, thereby ensuring maximum possible accuracy for the attack.

The snag in all this is, of course, that the 'Bear' itself is a huge and vulnerable target for hostile carrier-based interceptors or naval anti-aircraft missiles if it is spotted or picked up by the ships' radar. ECM jammers might help to protect it, but this seems to be an obvious instance of where we can expect to see large, piloted aircraft replaced eventually by small, remotely piloted vehicles (see pages 118–121). These could be launched from the missile ships, and could be so small that they might well escape detection by the targets' warning radars.

These last eight pages have emphasized the tremendous variety of fixed-wing aircraft that are employed for modern

The M-12 amphibian normally operates from shore bases, but has
the advantage of being able to fly also from water

anti-submarine and maritime reconnaissance duties, from
shore bases or harbours. It would be untrue to suggest that
the Japanese Shin Meiwa PS-1 is unique in belonging to the
flying-boat family. The Soviet Naval Air Force has about 100
Beriev M-12 Tchaikas with flying-boat hulls for operation
from water. However, these are amphibians, based ashore
and normally flown from runways. Much smaller than the
PS-1, they are nonetheless well-equipped and useful aircraft,
providing further evidence that flying-boats are not quite dead.

The entirely different RAF Nimrod, named after the 'mighty
hunter' in the first book of the Bible, is a far more formidable
proposition. It was the first MR aircraft to be powered by
turbofan engines, its four 12,000 lb (5,443 kg) Rolls-Royce
Speys enabling it to cruise to its patrol area at 490 mph (787
km/h) and then shut down two engines to save fuel and extend
its mission time to an impressive 12 hours. The airframe is
basically that of a Comet 4 airliner, with a large, unpressurised

lower-deck pannier attached under the standard fuselage to house some of the anti-submarine equipment and weapons. The cabin, designed originally for 101 passengers, provides ample room for the tactical displays and hunter/killer gear manned by the nine crew members who do not sit on the flight deck. This special equipment, some of it highly secret, reflects the leadership that Britain has always maintained in certain branches of electronics. Proof of this has been given by three wins by RAF Nimrods in four years in the annual contest for the coveted Fincastle Trophy for anti-submarine capability, against Orion, Argus and Neptune aircraft of the New Zealand, Canadian and Australian Air Forces. Far more than mere games, these contests – organized with full naval participation – are devised to test to the limit the ingenuity and skill of the crews engaged, leading to improvement in tactics and standards.

As well as operating independently, the Nimrod anti-submarine aircraft can work in conjunction with modern killer submarines

AIR POWER AFLOAT

Aeroplanes first went to sea on ships as aids to reconnaissance, to give the commander of a naval force eyes to see over the horizon. By the Second World War, they had advanced so much in weapon-carrying capability that key naval battles in the Pacific were fought entirely between carrier-based aircraft and enemy ships, out of sight of the opposing surface fleets. Sinkings were so heavy that carriers dominated the oceans; but it was their aircraft that did the damage, and air force leaders insisted that all big ships, including carriers, were obsolete once shore-based attack aircraft had the range to venture far out over the ocean and launch anti-shipping missiles beyond the reach of the fleet's own guns and missiles.

Obsolete or not, carriers played a major part in Korea and Vietnam, cruising off the coast and launching ceaseless strikes against targets ashore. They played significant roles in every confrontation from Suez in 1956 to Cuba in 1962 and the more recent blockade of Rhodesia. Financial, not strategic, considerations compelled the Royal Navy to scrap its large carriers one by one, and to abandon plans for replacements. By the mid-seventies only HMS *Ark Royal* remained in commission, with a reprieve until about 1978–79.

The US Navy continues to operate 14 big carriers, one of which, the 91,400-ton USS *Nimitz*, is the largest warship ever built. With an overall length of 1,092 ft (332 m) and a complement of about 100 aircraft, it is the traditional 'floating air base', able to launch everything from nuclear attack bombers to anti-submarine aircraft, fleet defence fighters and airborne early warning aircraft. More significant is the introduction of two completely new classes of aircraft carrier into the Soviet Navy, both designed for V/STOL aircraft and helicopters, with no apparent provision for catapults and arrester gear for conventional fixed-wing types. Even small ships can operate aircraft that are able to take off vertically, and few of the larger ships of the Royal Navy, in particular, lack accommodation for at least one such aircraft.

The great advantage of a carrier task force is its mobility,

Seasprite anti-submarine and anti-missile helicopter operating from a US Navy destroyer

Above Preparing to launch a heavily loaded A-7E by catapult from a large US Navy carrier

which enables it to carry its on-board mini air force speedily across the oceans of the world to within range of most likely targets. It enables naval strike aircraft to be comparatively small, as they need less fuel than land-based bombers which may have to fly 10,000 miles (16,000 km) to and from their targets. The smaller the fuel load that is carried, the greater the weight of weapons can be.

Illustrations on this page and opposite show two types of aircraft used by the US Navy for attack in the mid-seventies. The A-7E Corsair II, powered by an American-built Rolls-Royce turbofan, carries more than 15,000 lb (6,800 kg) of weapons on its underwing and fuselage racks. It is a sturdy, uncomplicated type which normally releases its weapons in a dive with great accuracy (as described for the USAF's A-7D version, on page 28). The twin-engined Grumman A-6 is even more interesting in view of the variants that have been evolved from the basic two-seat attack model.

In the picture opposite, the attack force of A-6E Intruders is led by a four-seat EA-6B Prowler loaded down with AN/ALQ-99 ECM equipment to jam enemy warning, gun and missile guidance radars. Another version, the A-6E TRAM (Target Recognition Attack Multisensor), carries infra-red and

Opposite A-6E Intruder strike force led by an EA-6B Prowler radar-jamming aircraft

laser equipment in an underfuselage turret to find its target and launch laser-guided weapons against it.

A naval force must be protected by anti-submarine aircraft. These cannot be provided satisfactorily from shore bases as the aircraft would waste too much time and fuel getting to and from a fleet in mid-ocean. Unfortunately, aircraft as large and fully equipped as the Nimrod and Orion could never be operated from the restricted deck of even the biggest carrier. This presents the designers of carrier-based anti-submarine aircraft with the problem of producing an aeroplane small enough to be operated at sea but big enough to carry the equipment essential to hunt and kill a modern submarine.

Although nobody would claim that the US Navy's twin-turbofan Lockheed S-3A Viking can do everything within the capability of a Nimrod, it is still a remarkable and efficient combat type. Less than half as long as a Nimrod and a quarter as heavy, with a crew of only four, it has self-contained inertial and Doppler navigation systems, a large search radar, a forward-looking infra-red (FLIR) scanner, MAD, ECM equipment, sonobuoys, and internal and external racks for an

Shown here on a steam catapult, the Viking can also make unassisted take-offs from the angled deck of a large carrier

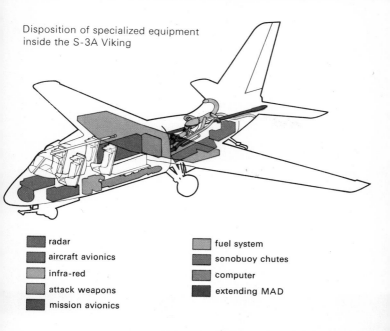

Disposition of specialized equipment inside the S-3A Viking

- ◼ radar
- ◼ aircraft avionics
- ◻ infra-red
- ◻ attack weapons
- ◼ mission avionics
- ◻ fuel system
- ◼ sonobuoy chutes
- ◻ computer
- ◼ extending MAD

immense range of weapons, including homing torpedoes, depth bombs, mines, cluster bombs and rockets.

Duties have to be worked out carefully with so much to be done by only four men. The pilot maintains command and control, while the tactical co-ordinator (tacco) is responsible for strategy and instructs the pilot on the manoeuvres necessary to ensure a successful attack on the target. The co-pilot, in addition to his flying duties, has to monitor the non-acoustic sensors, such as radar and infra-red. The acoustic sensor operator (senso), in the rear cabin with tacco, controls the sonobuoys and other acoustic sensors. All four have Escapac ejection seats of the latest zero-zero type, operable even while the aircraft is stationary at sea level. By the time they touched water, these seats could each produce and inflate a life raft to help the crewmen survive the emergency. Other safety aids, for non-routine use, include an automatic carrier landing system able to bring the Viking down on to the carrier deck at night or in bad weather.

An aircraft carrier can provide most of the facilities and services found at a land aerodrome; but it is still very small by comparison with an airport, and modern, high-performance aircraft have to be designed with great ingenuity if they are to be carrier-based.

Let us assume that a particular type of combat aircraft could take off from a land aerodrome when its speed along the runway reached 170 mph (275 km/h). If it has to take off from a carrier, the ship's forward speed of, say, 30 knots is a big help. If the ship sails into a 20 knot headwind, this puts a wind speed of 50 knots (57 mph, 92 km/h) over the deck and over the wings of the aeroplane before it begins its run. It is sufficient to enable many types of aircraft to make a normal, unassisted take-off by running forward the full length of the deck, which is more than 1,000 ft (305 m) long on a big American carrier. However, the difference between 57 mph and 170 mph is so

A Viking, with wings folded, being taken to the below-deck hangar of a large carrier by deck-side lift

great that our particular combat aircraft must be assisted into the air by one of the ship's steam catapults.

As a result, it needs a hook with which the catapult strop can tow it rapidly along the foredeck and into the air. While it is on its mission, the carrier will not only steam a considerable distance but may change course. This requires sophisticated navigation systems and other equipment in the aircraft if it is to find the ship. When it lands, the weather may have deteriorated, or it may be after dark. To help the aircraft make a safe touchdown on the small, moving airstrip, which may be rising and falling 30 ft (10 m) in a rough sea, ship and aircraft are equipped with automatic landing equipment. An arrester hook is needed to pick up the deck wires which drag the heavy aircraft to a sudden halt, thumping it onto the deck with a bone-shuddering jar.

Once down, the returned machine must be moved out of the way of other landing aircraft as rapidly as possible. As ground crew disengage the arrester hook, it taxies forward, folding its

By means of a 'buddy' pack, the pilot of an A-4 Skyhawk tops up the tanks of a colleague in flight

wings by an automatic, hydraulically-powered system as it goes. To make it a still smaller 'package', its nose might fold sideways and its tail-fin down. In the case of a helicopter, its blades would be folded back along the top of the fuselage and, perhaps, the whole tail might fold sideways and forward. Reduced in overall dimensions, the aircraft can now be taken down by lift into the limited space of the below-deck hangars.

Even these special features may not be enough. The aircraft may also need a boundary-layer control system which blows air back over its wings, flaps and tail to give greatly-improved 'lift' during take-off and landing. Its nosewheel leg may be able to extend for take-off, putting the wing at a greater angle to the deck and again improving lift. One US carrier-based fighter, the F-8 Crusader, even had a two-position wing, the leading-edge of which could be raised by hydraulic jack to increase the wing's 'angle of incidence' by 7 degrees. This improved lift at take-off and enabled the Crusader to land comparatively slowly without its long fuselage

needing to be nose-up. Although the idea worked well, it was not embodied on the A-7 Corsair II attack aircraft which was evolved from the F-8 with a shorter fuselage and fixed wing.

Some of the other special features of naval aircraft have been adopted for shore-based types. Many fighters, for example, now have a naval-type arrester hook to stop them should they over-run the end of the runway at a land base. In return, the 'shore-based' technique of flight refuelling was adopted gratefully by naval aircraft operators. Often it can make the difference between a safe landing and a 'ditching' in the sea if a pilot returns from a long-distance mission, short of fuel, to find that the carrier has steamed 150 miles (240 km) further away since he took off. To ease such problems, formations of naval aircraft often include machines fitted with 'buddy' packs containing fuel and a trailing hose through which one machine can top up the tanks of another.

On pages 84–85, we looked at America's E-3A AWACS aircraft and its Soviet counterpart, which provide early warning of enemy air attack and can direct fighters to intercept the raiders. This is another idea which 'land' air forces have copied from the navy. The first type of aircraft to enter front-line service with an overfuselage saucer radome was a development of the US Navy's Grumman S-2 Tracker anti-submarine aircraft known as the E-1B Tracer. When piston-engined types gave way to turbine-powered designs, the Tracer was replaced by another Grumman aeroplane, the E-2 Hawkeye. As carriers were generally much larger by the time it was ready for service in 1966, it could be larger than the Tracer, with a take-off weight of more than 51,000 lb (23,000 kg), two 4,910 hp T56 turboprops, and a 24 ft (7.32 m) diameter radome of a new type which rotated at a speed of 6 rpm in flight. To ensure maximum efficiency and yet conform with stowage restrictions on board ship, the radome was so designed that it could be raised and lowered $22\frac{1}{4}$ in (0·64 m), as required.

Teams of Hawkeyes fly lazy circles around the perimeter of a fleet at sea by day or night in all weathers. When they detect approaching aircraft or ships, they compute the targets' precise positions immediately, discover whether or not they are friendly, and present all essential data on three displays in the Combat Information Centre on board each Hawkeye. Fighters or attack aircraft can be directed to intercept enemy forces threatening the fleet long before they come near enough to launch or fire their weapons.

Countermeasures equipment is of special importance to the crews of this type of aircraft. The service they provide is so vital that they must always be primary targets for any attack force, and their vulnerability has increased with the perfection of air-to-air and surface-to-air anti-radiation missiles which home on the source of radar signal emissions.

A carrier at sea is a city in miniature, requiring most of the support services that the crew could expect ashore. It has its own newspaper and closed-circuit TV programmes, a hospital for those who are ill, shops, barbers and, of course, the all-important post office for mail to and from home. Except in a period of emergency, when the fleet's precise location must be kept as secret as possible and radio silence is essential, the carrier is in continuous contact with other ships and shore

An E-2C Hawkeye with a force of F-14A Tomcat fighters under its direction. Had the aircraft seen over the ships not been identified as friendly, the Tomcats would have intercepted them long ago

C-2A Greyhound Carrier On-board Delivery transport parked with its wings folded on the deck of a large carrier.

bases. It also benefits from a regular air shuttle service maintained by COD (Carrier On-board Delivery) aircraft.

Typical of such types is the US Navy's C-2A Greyhound which has the wings, tail, engines and undercarriage of the E-2 Hawkeye married to a big, roomy, new fuselage able to accommodate up to 39 men, 20 stretcher patients, or 10,000 lb (4,535 kg) of freight, supplies and mail. Twenty-five were built and the sight of one of them coming in to land on a carrier deck is a morale-booster for the entire fleet. Equipment, personnel and mail that it brings from shore are destined not only for the carrier, but will be distributed by helicopter and other means throughout the entire naval force.

Small helicopters are the maids-of-all-work at sea. They flit from ship to ship with men and cargo, landing on the decks of larger ships and hovering over smaller ones to collect or deliver their loads by cable and hoist. They can help to make the facilities of a carrier – particularly medical aid – available to the men of the smallest vessel in a task force. So versatile is a 'chopper' like the Seasprite that it can haul a ditched pilot from his dinghy one minute and set out soon afterwards with a pair of homing torpedoes clutched to its fuselage to investigate a suspicious submarine, or ferry the captain ashore, in full dress uniform, to attend an official reception when the fleet is off the coast of a friendly nation.

Once the Royal Air Force had demonstrated the capabilities of the Harrier V/STOL combat aircraft (see pages 32–33), it was inevitable that carrier-based squadrons should become interested. Years of operating helicopters, for an immense variety of tasks, has left naval forces in no doubt of the value of vertical take-off and landing. Unfortunately, helicopters are slow and no match for enemy jets in combat. So, at a time when once-

Kaman SH-2 Seasprite picking up a ditched fighter pilot from his dinghy at sea

The once-familiar 'batsman' of Second World War carrier operations can still be very helpful when guiding the pilot of a Harrier to a gentle touchdown on a small platform on a warship

great sea powers like Britain can no longer afford large carriers, it began to look as though the majority of naval air forces might be limited in future jobs like anti-submarine work with helicopters.

The Harrier offered a reprieve, needing no 1,000 ft (305 m) flight decks from which to operate and yet able to fly at around the speed of sound and survive in the same sky as enemy fighters, bombers and attack aircraft. First to find the courage and the cash to take an operational squadron of Harriers to sea was the US Marine Corps. Afterwards, it was so enthusiastic that it began seeking ways of obtaining even more effective versions, with a more powerful engine, greater weapon load and additional equipment.

The Royal Navy, too, began planning for Harrier operations from a completely new class of ship which it called a 'through-deck cruiser'. This can be regarded as a small carrier without the expensive and complicated catapults, arrester gear and other equipment needed to operate conventional fixed-wing aircraft. Or it could be thought of as a development of the Soviet type of helicopter cruiser, with a full deck instead of only a rear deck. Significantly, the first Soviet aircraft carriers, approaching completion in the mid-seventies, are 35,000-ton vessels intended, like the British through-deck cruiser, to carry a mixture of V/STOL jets and anti-submarine helicopters. There is little indication of the type of fixed-wing aircraft they will carry. The Royal Navy, on the other hand, has ordered an initial batch of 24 Harrier FRS. 1s, with a powerful new search radar in the nose and provision for carrying air-to-air missiles as well as attack weapons and reconnaissance equipment.

First V/STOL fighter to operate from the Soviet Navy's new aircraft carriers might be an improved version of the Yakovlev Yak-36, a rather crude, twin-jet experimental aircraft that was first demonstrated in public in 1967 and was tested subsequently from a specially-installed pad on the flight deck of the helicopter carrier *Moskva*

EYES IN THE SKY

Before the First World War, few military leaders imagined that the aeroplane could be of the slightest use to them except for reconnaissance in battle. Today aerial reconnaissance has evolved into one of the most effective ways of preventing war rather than simply of waging war. The SALT (Strategic Arms Limitation Talks) agreements concluded between America and the Soviet Union are dependent on both parties keeping their word, and deploying no more ICBMs and ABMs than are specified in the agreements. These lay down not only the permitted totals of each type of missile, but the kind of warheads that may be fitted. This is essential, as an ICBM carrying a single, large thermonuclear warhead in a conventional re-entry vehicle is very different from the same missile with a warhead comprising five or eight smaller H-bombs, each of which can be aligned to hit precisely a different target, manoeuvring to elude defensive ABMs as it does so.

The SALT agreements would never have been signed if both sides had to trust each other. When such trust exists, ICBMs will no longer be needed. Meanwhile, how can the USA and USSR be sure that the agreements are not broken? The answer is by means of reconnaissance satellites. Some modern reconnaissance satellites, like the USAF's Big Bird, are as large as two motor coaches placed end to end and weigh 11 tons. The cameras they carry provide pin-sharp pictures of objects smaller than 12 in (0.3 m) across, from heights above 100 miles (160 km). To avoid wasting film, the satellites are accompanied by small meteorological satellites which switch off the cameras if the target area is obscured by cloud. With such spacecraft in orbit, no missile site can be hidden and no missile can retain any secrets about its warhead.

On several occasions, Russia has demonstrated its ability to destroy one satellite in orbit with another as part of its continuous Cosmos space programme. But it would be in nobody's interest to destroy the reconnaissance satellites of East and West, bringing back the 'cold war' fear of the unknown.

Even in a space age, there are still many tasks that a piloted

A Cosmos interceptor satellite destroying another Cosmos in orbit

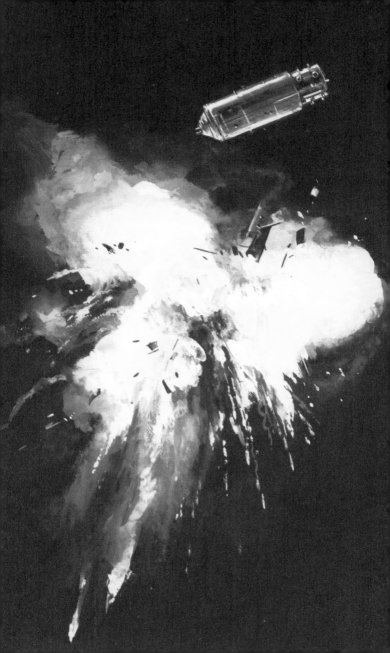

Tactical photographic-reconnaissance version of the Yak-28, recording damage to a recently attacked bridge

reconnaissance aircraft can do best. Except in the case of a geostationary satellite, fixed in orbit permanently over a selected point on Earth, a satellite can photograph a particular area only as it passes quickly overhead on successive orbits. An aeroplane, on the other hand, can be flown directly to anywhere and stay there as long as its fuel, its pilot's endurance or local opposition permit. In the days of more gentlemanly diplomacy, local permission was considered a prerequisite to a flight over somebody else's territory. The shooting down of Gary Powers' American U-2 spy-plane near Sverdlovsk, in the heart of the Soviet Union, on May Day 1960 is the most publicized of many incidents that reveal how much times have changed.

Lockheed's Mach 3 SR-71A, one of the most remarkable

aeroplanes ever built, has served with the USAF's 9th Strategic Reconnaissance Wing since 1966, and is believed to have made frequent overflights of Cuba, China up to 1971, Vietnam after the cessation of US bombing of the North, the Middle East after the Yom Kippur War of October 1973, and other 'sensitive' places. The likelihood of an SR-71A being shot down at a cruising height of up to 100,000 ft (30,500 m) is negligible – an immunity shared by the Soviet MiG-25s (NATO reporting name 'Foxbat-B') which have performed similar missions, with equal regularity, over areas like Northern Iran, Israel and the perimeter of the Warsaw Treaty nations in Europe.

The SR-71A, which is made largely of titanium and carries a crew of two dressed in spacesuits, is thought to be the fastest aeroplane that has ever operated with an air force. The MiG-25, which serves also in fighter form, is certainly the fastest combat aircraft yet introduced into squadron service. Other reconnaissance aircraft are typified by the camera-carrying Yak-28 (NATO 'Brewer'), which is intended for the more traditional forms of photographic mission in a front-line environment, and which exists also as an ECM jamming counterpart to the US Navy's EA-6B Prowler.

Satellites are permitted to make their reconnaissance flights

Lockheed's SR-71A, successor to the notorious U-2 spy-plane, is often known as the 'Blackbird' because of its overall black paint-scheme

Above Two Su-15 (NATO 'Flagon') interceptors investigate an elint-gathering EC-135 flying just outside territorial limits

without hindrance because they are the chosen inspection instruments of the SALT agreements. Aircraft like the SR-71A and MiG-25 survive because nothing is capable of catching them. The aeroplanes used for many electronic intelligence (elint) operations lack these advantages and a considerable number have been shot down, sometimes quite illegally while flying on their own side of an international border. Legalities are seldom observed in the rough, tough, cloak-and-dagger world of intelligence gathering.

The basic form of elint consists of flying as close as practicable to the territory of a potential enemy, 'listening' to every emission from his radios and radars to discover precisely what kind of equipment is in service, the frequencies on which it transmits, and how advanced it is. Such knowledge is vital when deciding the types of ECM devices that must be fitted to aircraft that might one day have to penetrate the defences in a particular sector of a common border. Aircraft employed for elint missions range from the Soviet Tu-16 and Tu-95 multi-engined bombers (see page 7) to the aerial-festooned RU-21J version of an off-the-shelf Beechcraft business twin and big C-135s, modified to carry special equipment in blisters and panniers that seem to be different on every aircraft.

Opposite Intelligence-gathering aerials on the Beechcraft RU-21J make it look as if it flew accidentally through a fence on take-off

Back in May 1965, the Chinese exhibited in Peking the remains of several aircraft which they claimed to have shot down during clandestine reconnaissance missions over their territory. The small swept-wing jets were clearly pilotless and bore a distinct resemblance to the Teledyne Ryan Model 124 Firebee drones which the US services use to provide realistic target practice for fighter pilots, anti-aircraft gunners and missile crews. For most people, this was the first hint of the existence of a completely new family of military aircraft known as remotely piloted vehicles (RPVs), to which brief reference has already been made on page 93.

Firebee targets can carry equipment to make them appear as large as B-52 bombers on radar scopes, equipment to provide heat sources on which infra-red missiles will home, to photograph missiles fired against them and to measure the distance by which the weapons miss them, as well as smaller, more expendable targets of various kinds which can be towed behind the Firebees at the end of a long cable. The Firebees can be ramp-launched from the ground or from a ship, or air-launched from under the wing of a DC-130 Hercules launch/director aircraft. They can be pre-programmed to fly a specific pattern, but are controlled normally by an operator on the ground or in the air by means of a small control box of the type used for a radio-controlled model.

The first modern reconnaissance RPVs, known as Ryan Model 147As, were little more than adaptations of the Firebee carrying highly advanced cameras, and launched and controlled in much the same way as the targets. More than 24 variants of the Model 147 have since been identified. Some have wings spanning only 13 ft (3.96 m) for high-speed, low-altitude missions; others have 32 ft (9.76 m) wings for high-altitude flying. Payloads include cameras, elint sensors, ECM jammers and 'chaff' dispensers to confuse enemy defensive and weapon radars. Guidance equipment can include a Doppler radar navigation system, forward-looking infra-red and TV links.

DC-130 launch/director aircraft of the USAF, at dusk, despatching Teledyne Ryan operational RPVs on clandestine reconnaissance sorties. Each returning RPV will deploy a parachute which will be snatched in mid-air by a recovery helicopter so that the RPV can be carried back to its base

Time after time, in places like Vietnam, the RPVs have brought back superb photographs of defence systems, targets before and after attack, and other scenes of significance to local field commanders. Their small size and high subsonic speed make them difficult targets for the defences; even when they are destroyed, no pilot is lost with them.

So good were the results achieved by RPVs that their makers, and the operators, began to study ways in which they might be of even greater service in war. One line of development led to a pair of designs by Boeing and Teledyne Ryan that were allocated the USAF code name 'Compass Cope'. Ryan's Model 235 spanned an impressive 81 ft 2 in (24·74 m), weighed 14,300 lb (6,486 kg) and was powered by a 4,050 lb (1,837 kg) thrust turbofan, mounted above the fuselage so that its heat would not be picked up so easily by infra-red missiles fired from below. Cruising speed could be as high as 400 mph (640 km/h), but 'Compass Cope' was intended primarily to orbit at 50,000–70,000 ft (15,250–21,350 m) for well over 24 hours at a time, replacing manned aircraft like the big EC-135

BGM-34 RPV launching a Maverick TV-guided missile against a ground target. While the RPV is being brought home, the missile will be steered to its target by an operator on the ground or in the launch aircraft

for elint missions and even keeping a watchful eye for other aircraft attempting to intrude into its airspace.

Simultaneously with work on this large RPV, Teledyne Ryan began experiments with variants of the Firebee/Model 147 equipped to carry 500 lb bombs, HOBOS TV-guided homing bombs, and Maverick missiles under their wings. Attacks against ground targets proved so promising that the USAF ordered a batch of improved models known as BGM-34s. Another important application was evolved during the Yom Kippur War in 1973, when the Israelis launched small Northrop Chukar target drones in advance of their strike forces of Phantom and Skyhawk jets to draw the fire of Arab surface-to-air missile batteries and so enable the piloted aircraft to follow through unscathed.

These are the kind of tasks that can be entrusted already to RPVs. The future may hold even more interesting possibilities. For example, the US Navy has matched a member of the Firebee family in an air-to-air dogfight with a Phantom fighter flown by a highly experienced combat crew. The Phantom fired its Sidewinder and Sparrow missiles against the RPV without hitting it; the drone several times put itself into such a position that it could have destroyed the Phantom had it been carrying missiles.

Military aviation has come a long way since the time when army commanders regarded tactical reconnaissance as the aircraft's only role. Technology has advanced at such a rate that it is man himself who is no longer good enough. Guided missiles, RPVs and spy satellites have replaced manned aircraft for many duties because they can think and react faster than a man, make high-g manoeuvres that no living body could withstand, and be sent on missions too hazardous or even suicidal for human aircrew.

However, such facts should be treated with caution. For example, a remotely piloted vehicle (RPV) does not dispense with a human pilot but simply transfers him from the 'hot seat' in the cockpit to the comparative safety of a control console on the ground or in a launch/director aircraft. Similarly, the information produced by a satellite must be assessed ultimately by human eyes and brains; if it reveals a need for immediate air operations, men trained to the highest standards will still be needed to fly the combat aircraft.

In fact, manned aircraft will soon replace rockets for one key military and scientific task, with consequent improvements in efficiency and cost. The illustration opposite shows the Space Shuttle orbiter which the Americans are developing for service towards the end of the 'seventies. Launched into orbit with the aid of two reusable booster rockets, it will make possible a wide range of activities. Individual satellites will be placed directly into orbit by space-walking crewmen or automatically. Others no longer working at peak efficiency will be retrieved for repair and servicing. Scientific tasks will be undertaken inside a space laboratory housed in the orbiter's payload bay.

The Space Shuttle orbiter will be a massive vehicle, 122 ft (37·19 m) long, with a span of 78 ft (23·77 m), and will land at an airfield, like a conventional aeroplane, when its work is done. At the moment, nobody imagines that it will be suitable for combat missions of any kind. Only the cynic may wish to recall that the aeroplane, too, began as an unarmed, unaggressive vehicle.

A crewman space-walks from a Space Shuttle orbiter to remove a film-pack from a reconnaissance satellite

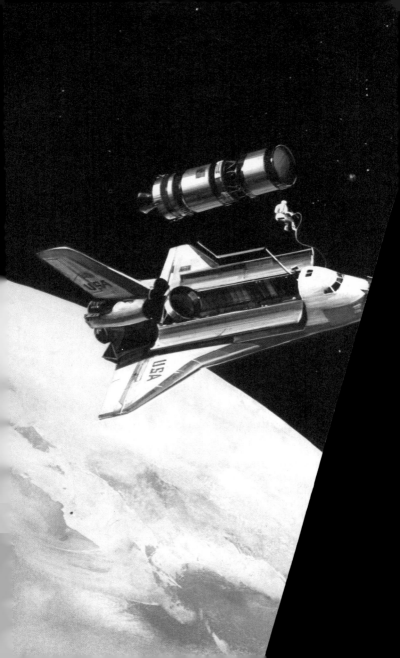

BOOKS TO READ

Photo Reconnaissance by Andrew J. Brookes; Ian Allan, Shepperton, 1975.

L'Homme, L'Air et L'Espace by Charles Dollfus, Henry Beaubois and Camille Rougeron; Editions de l'Illustration, Paris, 1965.

Aviation, an historical survey from its origins to the end of World War II by Charles H. Gibbs-Smith; Her Majesty's Stationery Office, London, 1970.

The Great Planes by James Gilbert; Paul Hamlyn, London, 1970.

Warplanes of the Third Reich by William Green; Macdonald, London, 1970.

Kitty Hawk to Concorde by H. F. King; Jane's Yearbooks, London, 1970.

The Spirit of St Louis by Charles A. Lindbergh; Charles Scribner's Sons, New York, 1953.

The Pocket Encyclopaedia of World Aircraft in Colour (series) by Kenneth Munson; Blandford Press, London, 1966–70.

British Aviation: The Pioneer Years and *British Aviation: The Great War and Armistice* by Harald Penrose; Putnam & Company Ltd, London, 1967/69.

Transport Aircraft since 1945 by John Stroud; Putnam & Company Ltd, London, 1966/68.

Aircraft by John W. R. Taylor; Hamlyn, London, 1970 (1974).

Aircraft of the World edited by John W. R. Taylor; Michael Joseph, London, 1969.

Air Facts and Feats by John W. R. Taylor, Michael Taylor and David Mondey; Guinness Superlatives, Enfield, 1973.

Warfare by John W. R. Taylor; Hamlyn, London,

Jane's All the World's Aircraft edited by John W. R. Taylor; London, annually.

*by John W. R. Taylor; Phoenix House,

Air Force (three volumes) by John W. R. Taylor; Ian Allan, Shepperton, 1968/70.

*Taylor and David Mondey; Ian Allan,

INDEX AND SPECIFICATIONS

Soviet data estimated. Illustrations in **bold** type. *Helicopter rotor diameter.

Type	Crew	Span*	Length	Max weight	Max speed	Page Numbers
Cessna A-37B Dragonfly	2	35 10½ (10·93)	28 3¼ (8·62)	14,000 (6,350)	507 (816)	**61**
Cessna T-37B	2	33 9¼ (10·30)	29 3 (8·92)	6,600 (2,993)	426 (685)	61
Dassault Mirage III-E	1	27 0 (8·22)	49 3½ (15·03)	29,760 (13,500)	1,460 (2,350)	40, **40**, 41 (includes Mirage 5)
Dassault Mirage F1-C	1	27 6¾ (8·40)	49 2½ (15·00)	32,850 (14,900)	1,460 (2,350)	41, **41**
Douglas A-1J Skyraider	1	50 9 (15·49)	38 10 (11·84)	25,000 (11,340)	318 (512)	24, 59
Fairchild A-10A	1	57 6 (17·53)	53 4 (16·26)	46,624 (21,148)	453 (729)	**24—25**, 25
General Dynamics F-111E	2	63 0ext (19·20)	73 6 (22·40)	91,500 (41,500)	1,650 (2,655)	22, **23**, 31, **82—83**
General Dynamics YF-16A	1	32 10 (10·01)	47 7¾ (14·52)	33,000 (14,968)	1,320+ (2,125+)	44, **44**, 45
Grumman A-6E Intruder	2	53 0 (16·15)	54 7 (16·64)	60,400 (27,397)	648 (1,043)	**98**, 99
Grumman C-2A Greyhound	3	80 7 (24·56)	56 8 (17·27)	54,830 (24,870)	352 (567)	108, **108**
Grumman E-2C Hawkeye	5	80 7 (24·56)	57 7 (17·55)	51,569 (23,391)	374 (602)	84, 106, **107**
Grumman EA-6B Prowler	4	53 0 (16·15)	59 5 (18·11)	58,500 (26,535)	600 (966)	**98**, 99
Grumman F-14A Tomcat	2	64 1½ext (19·54)	62 0 (18·89)	72,000 (32,658)	1,544 (2,485)	8, **8**, 36, **36**, 37, **107**
Handley Page Victor K.2	5	120 0 (36·6)	114 11 (35·0)	170,000+ (77,110+)	600+ (966+)	7, **7**
Hawker Siddeley Buccaneer S.2B	2	44 0 (13·41)	63 5 (19·33)	62,000 (28,123)	645 (1,038)	32
Hawker Siddeley Gnat T.1	2	24 0 (7·32)	37 10 (11·51)	8,077 (3,664)	627 (1,009)	**9**
Hawker Siddeley Harrier GR.3	1	25 3 (7·70)	45 6 (13·87)	25,000+ (11,339+)	737+ (1,186+)	32, **33**, 110, **110**, 111
Hawker Siddeley Nimrod MR.1	12	114 10 (35·00)	126 9 (38·63)	192,000 (87,090)	575 (926)	94, 95, **95**, 100
Hawker Siddeley Vulcan B.2	5	111 0 (33·83)	99 11 (30·45)	180,000+ (81,650+)	625+ (1,006+)	**17**, 32
Helio U-10D Courier	1	39 0 (11·89)	31 0 (9·45)	3,600 (1,633)	167 (269)	**64**, 65
Hindustan (HAL) Gnat Mk 1	1	22 2 (6·76)	29 9 (9·07)	8,885 (4,030)	714 (1,150)	42, **43**
Hughes YAH-64	2	48 0 (14·63)		13,600 (6,169)		53, **53**
Ilyushin Il-38		122 8½ (37·4)	129 10 (39·6)		400+ (645+)	92
Ilyushin Il-76	6	165 8 (50·50)	152 10½ (46·59)	346,125 (157,000)	528 (850)	66
Kaman SH-2D Seasprite	3	44 0 (13·41)		12,800 (5,805)	165 (265)	**97**, 109, **109**
Kamov Ka-25	3–4	51 8 (15·74)	32 0 (9·75)	16,100 (7,300)	137 (220)	**54**

Type	Crew	Span*	Length	Max weight	Max speed	Page Numbers
Lockheed C-5A Galaxy 5	5	222 8½ (67·88)	247 10 (75·54)	769,000 (348,810)	571 (919)	20, **76–77**, 76, 77, 78, **79**
Lockheed C-130H Hercules	4–5	132 7 (40·41)	97 9 (29·78)	175,000 (79,380)	386 (621)	11, **11**, **68–69**, 69, 70, 75, **79**, 118, **119** (all versions)
Lockheed F-104G Starfighter	1	21 11 (6·68)	54 9 (16·69)	28,779 (13,054)	1,450 (2,330)	42, **43**
Lockheed P-3C Orion	10	99 8 (30·37)	116 10 (35·61)	142,000 (64,410)	473 (761)	**90**, 91, **91**, 95, 100
Lockheed S-3A Viking	4	68 8 (20·93)	53 4 (16·26)	52,539 (23,831)	518 (834)	100, **100**, 101, **101**, **102–103**
Lockheed SR-71A 'Blackbird'	2	55 7 (16·95)	107 5 (32·74)	170,000 (77,110)	2,000+ (3,220+)	114, 115, **115**, 116
LTV A-7D Corsair II	1	38 9 (11·80)	46 1½ (14·06)	42,000 (19,050)	698 (1,123)	27, 28, 99, **99**, 105
McDonnell Douglas A-4M Skyhawk	1	27 6 (8·38)	40 3¼ (12·27)	24,500 (11,113)	645 (1,038)	**104–105**, 121
McDonnell Douglas F-4E Phantom II	2	38 5 (11·70)	63 0 (19·20)	57,400 (26,037)	1,450 (2,330)	7, **7**, 26, **26**, 32, **34**, 35, 121 (all versions)
McDonnell Douglas F-15A Eagle	1	42 9¾ (13·05)	63 9¾ (19·45)	40,000 (18,145)	1,650+ (2,655+)	36, 37, **37**
McDonnell Douglas YC-15	2	110 4 (33·63)	124 3 (37·88)	216,680 (98,285)	500 (805)	70, 72, 73, **72–73**
McDonnell Douglas/ Northrop F-18A	1	37 6 (11·43)	56 0 (17·07)	44,000 (20,000)	1,320+ (2,125+)	45
Mikoyan MiG-21MF	1	23 5½ (7·15)	51 8½ (15·76)	20,725 (9,400)	1,385 (2,230)	**42**, 43
Mikoyan MiG-23B	1	46 9ext (14·25)	55 1½ (16·80)	33,050 (15,000)	1,520 (2,450)	**30**
Mikoyan MiG-25	1	40 0 (12·20)	69 0 (21·00)	64,200 (29,120)	2,110 (3,400)	115
Mil Mi-24	2	55 9 (17·00)	55 9 (17·00)			52, **52**
Myasishchev M-4		165 7½ (50·48)	154 10 (47·20)	350,000 (158,750)	560 (900)	15, **17**, 92
North American T-6G	2	42 0 (12·80)	29 6 (8·99)	5,617 (2,548)	212 (341)	59
North American T-28D Trojan	2	40 7½ (12·38)	32 10 (10·00)	8,495 (3,853)	380 (611)	**58**, 59
Northrop Chukar I (RPV)	—	5 6¾ (1·69)	11 9 (3·58)	425 (192)	489 (787)	121
Northrop YF-17	1	35 0 (10·67)	56 0 (17·07)	23,000 (10,430)	1,320 (2,125)	44, 45, **45**
Panavia MRCA	2	45 7½ext (13·90)	54 9½ (16·70)	40,000 (18,145)	1,320+ (2,125+)	**31**, 32
PZL TS-11 Iskra 100	2	33 0¼ (10·07)	36 10¾ (11·25)	8,377 (3,800)	447 (720)	61

Type	Crew	Span*	Length	Max weight	Max speed	Page Numbers
Rockwell International B-1	4	137 0ext (41·75)	151 0 (46·03)	389,800 (176,815)	1,055 (1,700)	16, **18–19**, 20
Rockwell International Space Shuttle Orbiter	4	78 0 (23·77)	122 0 (37·18)	150,000 (68,000)		122, **123**
Saab 105G	2	31 2 (9·50)	35 5½ (10·80)	14,330 (6,500)	603 (970)	61
Saab AJ 37 Viggen	1	34 9¼ (10·60)	53 5¾ (16·30)	45,195 (20,500)	1,320 (2,125)	**38**, 39
Sepecat Jaguar GR.1	1	28 6 (8·69)	50 11 (15·52)	34,000 (15,500)	990 (1,593)	**29**, 30
Shin Meiwa PS-1	10	108 8¾ (33·14)	109 11 (33·50)	94,800 (43,000)	340 (547)	**86–87**, 87, 88, 94
Soko G2-A Galeb	2	38 1½ (11·62)	33 11 (10·34)	9,210 (4,178)	505 (812)	61
Soko P-2 Kraguj	1	34 11 (10·64)	26 0½ (7·93)	3,580 (1,624)	183 (295)	22, **23**, 24
Sukhoi Su-7B	1	29 3½ (8·93)	57 0 (17·37)	29,750 (13,500)	1,055 (1,700)	31
Sukhoi Su-15	1	30 0 (9·15)	68 0 (20·5)	35,275 (16,000)	1,650 (2,655)	**116**
Sukhoi Su-20	1	41 0ext (12·50)	56 0 (17·00)	29,750 (13,500)	1,055 (1,700)	32
Teledyne Ryan Model 124 Firebee I (RPV)	—	12 10¾ (3·93)	22 10¾ (6·98)	2,500 (1,134)	690 (1,112)	118, 121
Teledyne Ryan Model 147H (AQM-34N RPV)	—	32 0 (9·75)	30 0 (9·14)	3,820 (1,732)		118, **119** (incl. other versions)
Teledyne Ryan Model 234 (BGM-34B RPV)	—	14 6 (4·42)	26 0 (7·92)	3,230 (1,465)		**120–121**, 121
Teledyne Ryan Model 235 (YQM-98A Compass Cope R RPV)	—	81 2 (24·74)	38 4 (11·68)	14,300 (6,486)	400 (640)	120
Tupolev Tu-16	7	110 0 (33·5)	120 0 (36·5)	150,000 (68,000)	587 (945)	92, **93**, 116
Tupolev Tu-95		159 0 (48·50)	155 10 (47·50)	340,000 (154,220)	500 (805)	7, **7**, 15, **15** **17**, 92, **92**, 93, 116
Tupolev Tu-126		167 8 (51·10)	188 0 (57·30)			85, **85**
Westland Scout AH.1	2	32 3 (9·83)	30 4 (9·24)	5,300 (2,405)	131 (211)	**10**
Westland Sea King HAS.2	4	62 0 (18·90)	55 9¾ (17·01)	21,000 (9,525)	129 (208)	10, 55, **55**
Yakovlev Yak-28	2	42 6 (12·95)	71 0½ (21·65)	35,000 (15,875)	733 (1,180)	**114**, 115